Spinning Tops
and
Gyroscopic Motions

with 66 illustrations

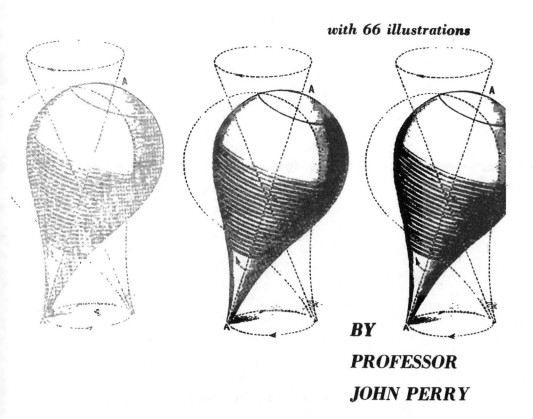

**BY
PROFESSOR
JOHN PERRY**

Manufactured in the United States of America.

PREFACE

THIS is not the lecture as it was delivered. Instead of two pages of letterpress and a woodcut, the reader may imagine that for half a minute the lecturer played with a spinning top or gyrostat, and occasionally ejaculated words of warning, admonition, and explanation towards his audience. A verbatim report would make rather uninteresting reading, and I have taken the liberty of trying, by greater fullness of explanation, to make up to the reader for his not having seen the moving apparatus. It has also been necessary in a treatise intended for general readers to simplify the reasoning, the lecture having been delivered to persons whose life experiences peculiarly fitted them for understanding scientific things. An "argument" has been added at the end to make the steps of the reasoning clearer.

JOHN PERRY.

Spinning Tops
and
Gyroscopic Motions

SPINNING TOPS

At a Leeds Board School last week, the master said to his class, "There is to be a meeting of the British Association in Leeds. What is it all about? Who are the members of the British Association? What do they do?" There was a long pause. At length it was broken by an intelligent shy boy. "Please, sir, I know—they spin tops!"[1]

Now I am sorry to say that this answer was wrong. The members of the British Association and the Operatives of Leeds have neglected top-spinning since they were ten years of age. If more attention were paid to the intelligent examination of the behaviour of tops, there would be greater advances in mechanical engineering and a great many industries. There would be a better general knowledge of astronomy. Geologists would not make mistakes by millions of years, and our knowledge of Light, and Radiant Heat, and other Electro-magnetic Phenomena would extend much more rapidly than it does.

I shall try to show you towards the end of the lecture that the fact of our earth's being a spinning body is one which would make itself known to us even if we lived in subterranean regions like the coming race of an ingenious novelist.[2] It is the greatest and most persistent cause of many of the phenomena which occur around us and beneath us, and it is probable that even Terrestrial Magnetism is almost altogether due to it. Indeed there is only one possible explanation of

---

[1] The *Operatives' Lecture* is always well advertised in the streets beforehand by large posters.

[2] Bulwer Lytton's *Coming Race*.

the *Vril-ya* ignorance about the earth's rotation. Their knowledge of mechanics and dynamics was immense; no member attending the meeting of the British Association can approach them in their knowledge of, I will not say, *Vril,* but even of quite vulgar electricity and magnetism; and yet this great race which expresses so strongly its contempt for Anglo-Saxon *Koom-Poshery* was actually ignorant of the fact that it had existed for untold generations inside an object that spins about an axis.

Can we imagine for one instant that the children of that race had never spun a top or trundled a hoop, and so had had no chance of being led to the greatest study of nature? No; the only possible explanation lies in the great novelist's never having done these things himself. He had probably as a child a contempt for the study of nature, he was a baby Pelham, and as a man he was condemned to remain in ignorance even of the powers of the new race that he had created.

The *Vril-ya* ignorance of the behaviour of spinning bodies existing as it does side by side with their deep knowledge of magnetism, becomes even more remarkable when it comes home to us that the phenomena of magnetism and of light are certainly closely connected with the behaviour of spinning bodies, and indeed that a familiar knowledge of the behaviour of such bodies is absolutely necessary for a proper comprehension of most of the phenomena occurring in nature. The instinctive craving to investigate these phenomena seems to manifest itself soon after we are able to talk, and who knows how much of the intellectual inferiority of woman is due to her neglect of the study of spinning tops; but alas, even for boys in the pursuit of top-spinning, the youthful mind and muscle are left with no other guidance than that which is supplied by the experience of young and not very scientific companions. I remember distinctly that there were many puzzling problems presented to me every day. There were tops which nobody seemed able to spin, and there were others, well prized objects, often studied in their behaviour and coveted as supremely valuable, that behaved well under the most unscientific treatment. And yet nobody, even the makers, seemed to know why one behaved badly and the other well.

I do not disguise from myself the fact that it is rather a difficult task to talk of spinning tops to men who have lost that skill which they wonder at in their children; that knowingness of touch and handling which gave them once so much power over what I fear to call inanimate nature. A problem which the child gives up as hopeless of solution, is seldom attacked again in maturer years; he drives his desire for knowledge into the obscure lumber-closets of his mind, and there it lies, with the accumulating dust of his life, a neglected and almost forgotten instinct. Some of you may think that this instinct only remains with those minds so many of which are childish even to the limit of life's span; and probably none of you have had the opportunity of seeing how the old dust rubs off from the life of the ordinary man, and the old desire comes back to him to understand the mysteries that surround him.

But I have not only felt this desire myself, I have seen it in the excited eyes of the crowd of people who stand by the hour under the dropping cherry-blossoms beside the red-pillared temple of Asakusa in the Eastern capital of Japan, watching the *tedzu-mashi* directing the evolutions of his heavily rimmed *Koma*. First he throws away from him his great top obliquely into the air and catches it spinning on the end of a stick, or the point of a sword, or any other convenient implement; he now sends it about quite carelessly, catching it as it comes back to him from all sorts of directions; he makes it run up the hand-rail of a staircase into a house by the door and out again by the window; he makes it travel up a great corkscrew. Now he seizes it in his hands, and with a few dexterous twists gives it a new stock of spinning energy. He makes it travel along a stretched string or the edge of a sword; he does all sorts of other curious things with his tops, and suddenly sinks from his masterful position to beg for a few coppers at the end of his performance.

How tame all this must seem to you who more than half forget your childish initiation into the mysteries of nature; but trust me, if I could only make that old top-spinner perform those magical operations of his on this platform, the delight of the enjoyment of beautiful motion would come back. Perhaps it is only in Japan that such an exhibition is possible; the land where the waving bamboo, and the circling hawk, and the undulating summer sea, and every beautiful motion of nature are looked upon with tenderness; and perhaps it is from Japan that we shall learn the development of our childish enthusiasm.

The devotees of the new emotional art of beautiful motion and changing colour are still in the main beggars like Homer, and they live in garrets like Johnson and Savage; but the dawn of a new era is heralded, or rather the dawn has already come, for Sir William Thomson's achievements in the study of spinning tops rank already as by no means the meanest of his great career.

If you will only think of it, the behaviour of the commonest spinning top is very wonderful. When not spinning you see that it falls

FIGURE 1

GYROSCOPIC MOTION

down at once, I find it impossible to balance it on its peg; but what a very different object it is when spinning; you see that it not only does not fall down, it offers a strange resistance when I strike it, and actually lifts itself more and more to an upright position. Once started on scientific observation, nature gives us facts of an analogous kind in great plenty.

Those of you who have observed a rapidly moving heavy belt or rope, know that rapid motion gives a peculiar quasi-rigidity to flexible and even to fluid things.

Here, for example is a disc of quite thin paper (Fig. 1), and when I set it in rapid rotation you observe that it resists the force exerted by my hand, the blow of my fist, as if it were a disc of steel. Hear how it resounds when I strike it with a stick. Where has its flexibility gone?

Here again is a ring of chain which is quite flexible. It seems ridiculous to imagine that this could be made to stand up like a stiff hoop, and yet you could observe that when I give it a rapid rotation

FIGURE 2

SPINNING TOPS

on this mandril and let it slide off upon the table, it runs over the table just as if it were a rigid ring, and when it drops on the floor it rebounds like a boy's hoop (Fig. 2).

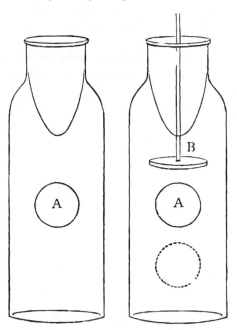

FIGURE 3[1]

Here again is a very soft hat, specially made for this sort of experiment. You will note that it collapses to the table in a shapeless mass when I lay it down, and seems quite incapable of resisting forces which tend to alter its shape. In fact, there is almost a complete absence of rigidity; but when this is spun on the end of a stick, first note how it has taken a very easily defined shape; secondly, note how it runs along the table as if it were made of steel; thirdly, note how all at once it collapses again into a shapeless heap of soft material when its rapid motion has ceased. Even so you will see that when a drunken man is not leaning against a wall or lamp-post, he feels

[1] The glass vessel ought to be broader in comparison with its height.

that his only chance of escape from ignominious collapse is to get up a decent rate of speed, to obtain a quasi-sobriety of demeanour by rapidity of motion.

The water inside this glass vessel (Fig. 3) is in a state of rapid motion, revolving with the vessel itself. Now observe the piece of paraffin wax A immersed in the water, and you will see when I push at it with a rod that it vibrates just as if it were surrounded with a thick jelly. Let us now apply Prof. Fitzgerald's improvement on this experiment of Sir William Thomson's. Here is a disc B stuck on the end of the rod; observe that when I introduce it, although it does not touch A, A is repelled from the disc. Now observe that when I twirl the disc it seems to attract A.

At the round hole in front of this box a rapid motion is given to a small quantity of air which is mixed with smoke that you may see it. That smoke-ring moves through the air almost like a solid body for a considerable distance unchanged, and I am not sure that it may not be possible yet to send as a projectile a huge poisoned smoke-ring, so that it may destroy or stupefy an army miles away. Remember that it is really the same air all the time. You will observe that two smoke-rings sent from two boxes have curious actions upon one another, and the study of these actions has given rise to Thomson's smoke-ring or vortex theory of the constitution of matter (Fig. 4).

FIGURE 4

SPINNING TOPS

It was Rankine, the great guide of all engineers, who first suggested the idea of molecular vortices in his explanations of heat phenomena and the phenomena of elasticity—the idea that every particle of matter is like a little spinning top; but I am now speaking of Thomson's theory. To imagine that an atom of matter is merely a curiously shaped smoke-ring formed miraculously in a perfect fluid, and which can never undergo permanent alteration, looks to be a very curious and far-fetched hypothesis. But in spite of certain difficulties, it is the foundation of the theory which will best explain most of the molecular phenomena observed by philosophers. Whatever be the value of the theory, you see from these experiments that motion does give to small quantities of fluid curious properties of elasticity, attraction and repulsion; that each of these entities refuses to be cut in two; that you cannot bring a knife even near the smoke-ring; and that what may be called a collision between two of them is not very different in any way from the collision between two rings of india-rubber.

Another example of rigidity given to a fluid by rapid motion, is the feeling of utter helplessness which even the strongest swimmers sometimes experience when they get caught in an eddy underneath the water.

I could, if I liked, multiply these instances of the quasi-rigidity which mere motion gives to flexible or fluid bodies. In Nevada a jet of water like the jet from a fireman's hose, except that it is much more rapid, which is nearly as easily projected in different directions, is used in mining, and huge masses of earth and rock are rapidly disintegrated by running water, which seems to be rather like a bar of steel than a jet of water in its rigidity.

It is, however, probable that you will take more interest in this box of brass which I hold in my hands. You see nothing moving, but really, inside this case there is a fly-wheel revolving rapidly. Observe that I rest this case on the table on its sharp edge, a sort of skate, and it does not tumble down as an ordinary box would do, or as this box will do after a while, when its contents come to rest. Observe that I can strike it violent blows, and it does not seem to budge from its vertical position; it turns itself just a little round, but does not get tilted, however hard I strike it. Observe that if I do get it tilted a little it does not fall down, but slowly turns with what is called a precessional motion (Fig. 5).

FIGURE 5

You will, I hope, allow me, all through this lecture, to use the term *precessional* for any motion of this kind. Probably you will object more strongly to the great liberty I shall take presently, of saying that the case *precesses* when it has this kind of motion; but I really have almost no option in the matter, as I must use some verb, and I have no time to invent a less barbarous one.

When I hold this box in my hands (Fig. 6), I find that if I move it with a motion of mere translation in any direction, it feels just as it would do if its contents were at rest, but if I try to turn it in my hands I find the most curious great resistance to such a motion. The result is that when you hold this in your hands, its readiness to move so long as it is not turned round, and its great resistance to turning round, and its unexpected tendency to turn in a different way from that in which you try to turn it, give one the most uncanny sensations. It seems almost as if an invisible being had hold of the box and

SPINNING TOPS

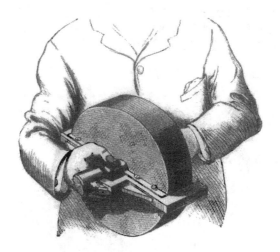

FIGURE 6

exercised forces capriciously. And indeed there is a spiritual being inside, what the algebraic people call an impossible quantity, what other mathematicians call "an operator."

Nearly all the experiments, even the tops and other apparatus you have seen or will see to-night, have been arranged and made by my enthusiastic assistant, Mr. Shepherd. The following experiment is not only his arrangement; even the idea of it is his. He said, you may grin and contort your body with that large gyrostat in your hands, but many of our audience will simply say to themselves that you only *pretend* to find a difficulty in turning the gyrostat. So he arranged this pivoted table for me to stand upon, and you will observe that when I now try to turn the gyrostat, it will not turn; however I may exert myself, it keeps pointing to that particular corner of the room, and all my efforts only result in turning round my own body and the table, but not the gyrostat.

Now you will find that in every case this box only resists having the axis of revolution of its hidden fly-wheel turned round, and if you are interested in the matter and make a few observations, you will soon see that every spinning body like the fly-wheel inside this case

GYROSCOPIC MOTION

resists more or less the change of direction of its spinning axis. When the fly-wheels of steam-engines and dynamo machines and other speed machines are rotating on board ship, you may be quite sure that they offer a greater resistance to the pitching or rolling or turning of the ship, or any other motion which tends to turn their axes in direction, than when they are not rotating.

Here is a top lying on a plate, and I throw it up into the air; you will observe that its motion is very difficult to follow, and nobody could predict, before it falls, exactly how it will alight on the plate; it may come down peg-end foremost, or hindmost, or sideways. But when I spin it (Fig. 7), and now throw it up into the air, there is no doubt whatever as to how it will come down. The spinning axis keeps parallel to itself, and I throw the top up time after time, without disturbing much the spinning motion.

If I pitch up this biscuit, you will observe that I can have no certainty as to how it will come down, but if I give it a spin before it leaves my hand there is no doubt whatever (Fig. 8). Here is a hat. I throw it up, and I cannot be sure as to how it will move, but if I

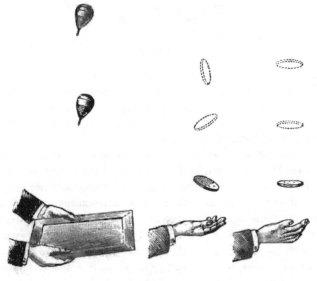

FIGURE 7-8

give it a spin, you see that, as with the top and the biscuit, the axis about which the spinning takes place keeps parallel to itself, and we have perfect certainty as to the hat's alighting on the ground brim downwards (Fig. 9).

FIGURE 9

I need not again bring before you the very soft hat to which we gave a quasi-rigidity a few minutes ago; but you will remember that my assistant sent that off like a projectile through the air when it was spinning, and that it kept its spinning axis parallel to itself just like this more rigid hat and the biscuit.

I once showed some experiments on spinning tops to a coffee-drinking, tobacco-smoking audience in that most excellent institution, the Victoria Music Hall in London. In that music hall, things are not very different from what they are at any other music hall except in beer, wine, and spirits being unobtainable, and in short scientific addresses being occasionally given. Now, I impressed my audience as strongly as I could with the above fact, that if one wants to throw a quoit with certainty as to how it will alight, one gives it a spin; if one wants to throw a hoop or a hat to somebody to catch upon a stick, one gives the hoop or hat a spin; the disinclination of a spinning body to let its axis get altered in direction can always be depended upon. I told them that this was why smooth-bore guns cannot be depended upon for accuracy;[1] that the spin which an ordinary bullet took depended greatly on how it chanced to touch the muzzle as it just left the gun, whereas barrels are now rifled, that is, spiral grooves are now cut inside the barrel of a gun and excrescences from the bullet or projectile fit into these grooves, so that as it is forced along the barrel of the gun by the explosive force of the powder, it must also spin about its axis. Hence it leaves motion about which there can be no doubt, and we know too that Fig. 10 shows the kind of motion which it has afterwards, for,

FIGURE 10

just like the hat or biscuit, its spinning axis keeps nearly parallel to itself. Well, this was all I could do, for I am not skilful in throwing hats or quoits. But after my address was finished, and after a young lady in a spangled dress had sung a comic song, two jugglers came upon the stage, and I could not have had better illustrations of the above principle than were given in almost every trick performed by this lady and gentleman. They sent hats, and hoops, and plates, and umbrellas spinning from one to the other. One of them threw a stream of knives into the air, catching them and throwing them up again with perfect precision and my now educated audience shouted with delight, and showed in other unmistakable ways that they observed the spin which that juggler gave to every knife as it left his hand, so that he

[1] In 1746 Benjamin Robins taught the principles of rifling as we know them now. He showed that the *spin* of the round bullet was the most important thing to consider. He showed that even the bent barrel of a gun did not deflect the bullet to anything like the extent that the spin of the bullet made it deflect in the opposite direction.

might have a perfect knowledge as to how it would come back to him again (Fig. 11). It struck me with astonishment at the time that almost without exception, every juggling trick performed that evening was an illustration of the above principle. And now, if you doubt my statement, just ask a child whether its hoop is more likely to tumble down when it is rapidly rolling along, or when it is going very slowly; ask a man on a bicycle to go more and more slowly to see if he keeps his balance better; ask a ballet-dancer how long she could stand on one toe without balancing herself with her arms or a pole, if she were not

FIGURE 11

spinning; ask astronomers how many months would elapse before the earth would point ever so far away from the pole star if it were not spinning; and above all, ask a boy whether his top is likely to stand upright upon its peg when it is not spinning as when it is spinning.

FIGURE 12

We will now examine more carefully the behaviour of this common top (Fig. 12). It is not spinning, and you observe that it tumbles down at once; it is quite unstable if I leave it resting upright on its peg. But now note that when it is spinning, it not only will remain upright resting on its peg, but if I give it a blow and so disturb its state, it goes circling round with a precessional motion which grows gradually less and less as time goes on, and the top lifts itself to the upright position again. I hope you do not think that time spent in careful observation of a phenomenon of this kind is wasted. Educated observation of the commonest phenomena occuring in our everyday life is never wasted, and I often feel that if workmen, who are the persons most familiar with inorganic nature, could only observe and apply simple scientific laws to their observations, instead of a great discovery every century we should have a great discovery every year. Well, to return to our top; there are two very curious observations to make. Please neglect for a short time the slight wobbling motions that occur. One observation we make is, that the top does not at first bow down in the direction of the blow. If I strike towards the south, the top bows towards the west; if I strike towards the west, the top bows down towards the north. Now the reason of this is known to all scientific men, and the principle underlying the top's behaviour is of very great importance in many ways, and I hope to make it clear to you. The second fact, that the top gradually reaches its upright position again, is one known to everybody, but the reason for it is not by any means well known, although I think that you will have no great difficulty in understanding it.

The first phenomenon will be observed in this case which I have

SPINNING TOPS

already shown you. This case (Fig. 5), with the fly-wheel inside it, is called a *gyrostat*. When I push the case it does not bow down, but slowly turns round. This gyrostat will not exhibit the second phenomenon; it will not rise up again if I manage to get it out of its upright position, but, on the contrary, will go precessing in wider and wider circles, getting further and further away from its upright position.

The first phenomenon is most easily studied in this balanced gyrostat (Fig. 13). You here see the fly-wheel G in a strong brass frame F, which is supported so that it is free to move about the vertical axis A B, or about the horizontal axis C D. The gyrostat is balanced by a weight W. Observe that I can increase the leverage of W or diminish it by shifting the position of the sleeve at A so that it will tend to either lift or lower the gyrostat, or exactly balance it as it does now. You must observe exactly what it is that we wish to study. If I endeavour to push F downwards, with the end of this stick (Fig. 14), it really moves horizontally to the right; now I push it to the right

FIGURE 13

(Fig. 15), and it only rises; now push it up, and you see that it goes to the left; push it to the left, and it only goes downwards. You will notice that if I clamp the instrument so that it cannot move vertically, it moves at once horizontally; if I prevent mere horizontal motion it readily moves vertically when I push it. Leaving it free as before, I will now shift the position of the weight W, so that it tends continu-

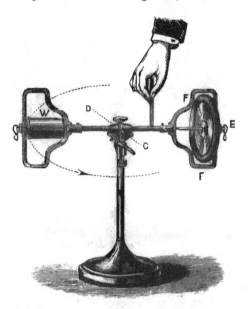

FIGURE 14

ally to lift the gyrostat, and of course the instrument does not lift, it moves horizontally with a slow precessional motion. I now again shift the weight W, so that the gyrostat would fall if it were not spinning (Fig. 16), and it now moves horizontally with a slow precessional motion which is in a direction opposed to the last. These phenomena are easily explained, but, as I said before, it is necessary first to observe them carefully. You all know now, vaguely, the fundamental fact. It is that if I try to make a very quickly spinning body change the direction of its axis, the direction of the axis will change, but not in the way I intended. It is even more curious than my countryman's pig, for when he wanted the pig to go to Cork, he had to pretend that he was driving the pig home. His rule was a very simple one, and we must find a rule for our spinning body, which is rather like a crab, that will only go along the road when you push it sidewise.

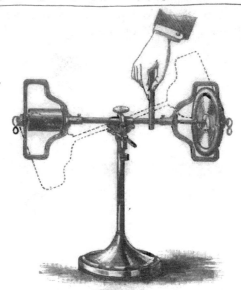

FIGURE 15

As an illustration of this, consider the spinning projectile of Fig. 10. The spin tends to keep its axis always in the same direction. But there is a defect in the arrangement, which you are now in a position to understand. You see that at A the air must be pressing upon the under-surface A A, and I have to explain that this pressure tends to make the projectile turn itself broadside on to the air. A boat in a current not allowed to move as a whole, but tied at its middle, sets itself broadside on to the current. Observe this disc of cardboard which I drop through the air edgewise, and note how quickly it sets itself broadside on and falls more slowly; and some of you may have thrown over into the water at Aden small pieces of silver for the diving boys, and you are aware that if it were not for this slow falling of the coins with a wobbling motion broadside on, it would be nearly impossible for any diving boy to get possession of them. Now all this is a parenthesis. The pressure of the air tends to make the projectile turn broadside on, but as the projectile is spinning it does not tilt up, no more than this gyrostat does when I try to tilt it up it really tilts out of the plane of the diagram, out of the plane of its flight; and only that artillerymen know exactly what it will do, this kind of *windage* of the projectile would give them great trouble.

You will notice that an experienced child when it wants to change the direction of a hoop, just exerts a tilting pressure with its hoopstick. A man on a bicycle changes his direction by leaning over so as to be out of balance. It is well to remind you, however, that the motion of a bicycle and its rider is not all rotational, so that it is not altogether the analogue of a top or gyrostat. The explanation of the swerv-

FIGURE 16

ing from a straight path when the rider tilts his body, ultimately comes to the same simple principle, Newton's second law of motion, but it is arrived at more readily. It is for the same reason—put briefly, the exercise of a centripetal force—that when one is riding he can

[1] NOTE.—In Fig. 16 the axis is shown inclined, but, only that it would have been more troublesome to illustrate, I should have preferred to show the precession occurring when the axis keeps horizontal.

FIGURE 10

materially assist his horse to turn a corner quickly, if he does not mind appearances, by inclining his body towards the side to which he wants to turn; and the more slowly the horse is going the greater is the tendency to turn for a given amount of tilting of one's body. Circus-riders, when galloping in a circle, assist their horses greatly by the position of their bodies; it is not to save themselves from falling by centrifugal force that they take a position on a horse's back which no riding-master would allow his pupil to imitate; and the respectable riders of this country would not scorn to help their horses in this way to quick turning movements, if they had to chase and collect cattle like American cowboys.

Very good illustrations of change of direction are obtained in playing *bowls*. You know that a bowl, if it had no *bias*, that is, if it had no little weight inside it tending to tilt it, would roll along the bowling-green in a straight path, its speed getting less and less till it stopped. As a matter of fact, however, you know that at the beginning, when it is moving fast, its path is pretty straight, but because it always has bias the path is never quite straight, and it bends more and more rapidly as the speed diminishes. In all our examples the slower the spin the quicker is the precession produced by given tilting forces.

Now close observation will give you a simple rule about the behaviour of a gyrostat. As a matter of fact, all that has been incomprehensible or curious disappears at once, if instead of speaking of this gyrostat as moving up or down, or to the right or left, I speak of its motions about its various axes. It offers no resistance to mere motion of translation. But when I spoke of its moving horizontally, I ought to have said that it moved about the vertical axis A B, (Fig. 13). Again,

FIGURE 17

what I referred to as up and down motion of F is really motion in a vertical plane about the horizontal axis C D. In future, when I speak of trying to give motion to F, think only of the axis about which I try to turn it, and then a little observation will clear the ground.

Here is a gyrostat (Fig. 17), suspended in gymbals so carefully that neither gravity nor any frictional forces at the pivots constrain it; nothing that I can do to this frame which I hold in my hand will affect the direction of the axis E F of the gyrostat. Observe that I whirl round on my toes like a ballet-dancer while this is in my hand. I move it about in all sorts of ways, but if it was pointing to the pole star at the beginning it remains pointing to the pole star; if it pointed towards the moon at the beginning it still points towards the moon. The fact is, that as there is almost no frictional constraint at the pivots there are almost no forces tending to turn the axis of rotation of the gyrostat, and I can only give it motions of translation. But now I will clamp this vertical spindle by means of a screw and repeat my ballet-dance whirl; you will note that I need not whirl round, a very small portion of a whirl is enough to cause this gyrostat (Fig. 18) to set its spinning axis vertical, to set its axis parallel to the vertical axis of rotation which I give it. Now I whirl in the opposite direction, the gyrostat at once turns a somersault, turns completely round and remains again with its axis vertical, and if you were to carefully note the direction of the spinning of the gyrostat, you would find the following rule to be generally true:—Pay no attention to meer translational motion, think only of rotation about axes, and just remember that when you constrain the axis of a spinning body to rotate, it will endeavour to set its own axis parallel to the new axis about which you

FIGURE 18

rotate it; and not only is this the case, but it will endeavour to have the direction of its own spin the same as the new rotation. I again twirl on my toes, holding this frame, and now I know that to a person looking down upon the gyrostat and me from the ceiling, as I revolved in the direction of the hands of a clock, the gyrostat is spinning in the direction of the hands of a clock; but if I revolve against the clock direction (Fig. 19) the gyrostat tumbles over so as again to be revolving in the same direction as that in which I revolve.

This then is the simple rule which will enable you to tell beforehand how a gyrostat will move when you try to turn it in any particular direction. You have only to remember that if you continued your

GYROSCOPIC MOTION

effort long enough, the spinning axis would become parallel to your new axis of motion, and the direction of spinning would be the same as the direction of your new turning motion.

Now let me apply my rule to this balanced gyrostat. I shove it, or give it an impulse downwards, but observe that this really means a rotation about the horizontal axis C D (Fig. 13), and hence the gyrostat turns its axis as if it wanted to become parallel to C D. Thus, looking down from above (as shown by Fig. 20), O E was the direction of the spinning axis, O D was the axis about which I endeavoured to move it, and the instantaneous effect was that O E altered to the position O G. A greater impulse of the same kind would have caused the spinning axis instantly to go to O H or O J, whereas an upward opposite impulse would have instantly made the spinning axis point in the direction O K, O L or O M, depending on how great the impulse was and the rate of spinning. When one observes these phenomena for the first time, one says, "I shoved it down, and it moved to the right; I shoved it up, and it moved to the left;" but if the direction of the spin were opposite to what it is, one would say, "I shoved it down, and

FIGURE 19

it moved to the left; I shoved it up, and it moved to the right." The simple statement in all cases ought to be, "I wanted to rotate it about a new axis, and the effect was to send its spinning axis towards the direction of the new axis." And now if you play with this balanced gyrostat as I am doing, shoving it about in all sorts of ways, you will find the rule to be a correct one, and there is no difficulty in predicting what will happen.

If this rule is right, we see at once why precession takes place. I put this gyrostat (Fig. 13) out of balance, and if it were not rotating it would fall downwards; but a force acting downwards really causes the gyrostat to move to the right, and so you see that it is continually moving in this way, for the force is always acting downwards, and the spinning axis is continually chasing the new axes about which gravity tends continually to make it revolve. We see also why it is that if the

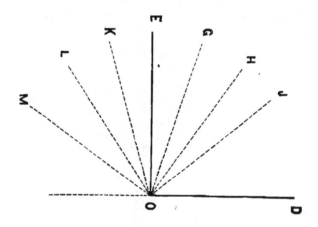

FIGURE 20

want of balance is the other way, if gravity tends to lift the gyrostat, the precession is in the opposite direction. And in playing with this gyrostat as I do now, giving it all sorts of pushes, one makes other observations and sees that the above rule simplifies them all; that is, it enables us to remember them. For example, if I use this stick to hurry on the precession, the gyrostat moves in opposition to the force which causes the precession. I am particularly anxious that you should remember this. At present the balance-weight is so placed that the gyrostat would fall if it were not spinning. But it is spinning, and so it precesses. If gravity were greater it would precess faster, and it comes home to us that it is this precession which enables the force of gravity to be inoperative in mere downward motion. You see that if the precession is hurried, it is more than sufficient to balance gravity, and the gyrostat rises. If I retard the precession, it is unable to balance gravity, and the gyrostat falls. If I clamp this vertical axis so that precession is impossible, you will notice that the gyrostat falls just as if it were not spinning. If I clamp the instrument so that it cannot move vertically, you notice how readily I can make it move horizontally; I can see it rotating horizontally like any other ordinary body.

In applying our rule to this top, observe that the axis of spinning is the axis E F of the top (Fig. 12). As seen in the figure, gravity is tending to make the top rotate about the axis F D, and the spinning axis in its chase of the axis F D describes a cone in space as it precesses. This gyrostat, which is top-heavy, rotates and precesses in much the same way as the top; that is, if you apply our rule, or use your observation, you will find that to an observer above the table the spinning and precession occur in the same direction, that is, either both with the hands of a watch, or both against the hands of a watch. Whereas, a top like this before you (Fig. 21), supported above its centre of gravity, or the gyrostat here (Fig. 22), which is also supported above its centre of gravity, or the gyrostat shown in Fig. 56, or any other gyrostat supported in such a way that it would be in stable equilibrium if it were not spinning; in all these cases, to an observer placed above the table, the precession is in a direction opposite to that of the spinning.

If an impulse be given to a top or gyrostat in the direction of the precession, it will rise in opposition to the force of gravity, and should at any instant the precessional velocity be greater than what it ought

SPINNING TOP

to be for the balance of the force of gravity, the top or gyrostat will rise, its precessional velocity diminishing. If the precessional velocity is too small, the top will fall, and as it falls the precessional velocity increases.

Now I say that all these facts, which are mere facts of observation,

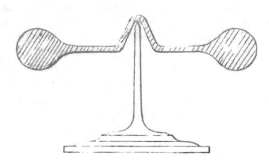

FIGURE 21-22

agree with our rule. I wish I dare ask you to remember them all. You will observe that in this wall sheet I have made a list of them. I speak of gravity as causing the precession, but the forces may be any others than such as are due to gravity.

WALL SHEET

1. RULE. When forces act upon a spinning body, tending to cause rotation about any other axis than the spinning axis, the spinning axis sets itself in better agreement with the new axis of rotation. Perfect

agreement would mean perfect parallelism, the directions of rotation being the same.

II. Hurry on the precession, and the body rises in opposition to gravity.

III. Delay the precession and the body falls, as gravity would make it do if it were not spinning.

IV. A common top precesses in the same direction as that in which it spins.

V. A top supported above its centre of gravity, or a body which would be in stable equilibrium if not spinning, precesses in the opposite direction to that of its spinning.

VI. The last two statements come to this:—When the forces acting on a spinning body tend to make the *angle* of precession greater, the precession is in the same direction as the spinning, and *vice versa*.

Having by observation obtained a rule, every natural philosopher tries to make his rule a rational one; tries to explain it. I hope you know what we mean when we say that we explain a phenomenon; we really mean that we show the phenomenon to be consistent with other better known phenomena. Thus when you unmask a spiritualist and show that the phenomena exhibited by him are due to mere sleight-of-hand and trickery, you explain the phenomena. When you show that they are all consistent with well-observed and established mesmeric influences, you are also said to explain the phenomena. When you show that they can be effected by means of telegraphic messages, or by reflection of light from mirrors, you explain the phenomena, although in all these cases you do not really know the nature of mesmerism, electricity, light, or moral obliquity.

The meanest kind of criticism is that of the man who cheapens a scientific explanation by saying that the very simplest facts of nature are unexplainable. Such a man prefers the chaotic and indiscriminate wonder of the savage to the reverence of a Sir Isaac Newton.

The explanation of our rule is easy. Here is a gyrostat (Fig. 23) something like the earth in shape, and it is at rest. I am sorry to say that I am compelled to support this globe in a very visible manner by gymbal rings. If this globe were just floating in the air, if it had no tendency to fall, my explanation would be easier to understand, and I could illustrate it better experimentally. Observe the point P.

If I move the globe slightly about the axis A, the point P moves to Q. But suppose instead of this that the globe and inner gymbal ring had been moved about the axis B; the point P would have moved to R.

FIGURE 23

Well, suppose both those rotations took place simultaneously. You all know that the point P would move neither to Q nor to R, but it would move to S; P S being the diagonal of the little parallelogram. The resultant motion then is neither about the axis O A in space, nor about the axis O B, but it is about some such axis as O C.

To this globe I have given two rotations simultaneously. Suppose a little being to exist on this globe which could not see the gymbals, but was able to observe other objects in the room. It would say that the direction of rotation is neither about O A nor about O B, but that the real axis of its earth is some line intermediate, O C in fact.

If then a ball is suddenly struck in two different directions at the same instant, to understand how it will spin we must first find how much spin each blow would produce if it acted alone, and about what axis. A spin of three turns per second about the axis O A (Fig. 24), and a spin of two turns per second about the axis O B, really mean that, the ball will spin about the axis O C with a spin of three and a half turns per second. To arrive at this result, I made O A, 3 feet long (any other scale of representation would have been right). and O B, 2 feet long, and I found the diagonal O C of the parallelogram shown on the figure to be 3½ feet long.

Observe that if the rotation about the axis O A is *with* the hands of a watch looking from O to A, the rotation about the axis O B looking from O to B, must also be with the hands of a watch, and the resultant rotation about the axis O C is also in a direction with the hands of a watch looking from O to C. Fig. 25 shows in two diagrams how necessary it is that on looking from O along either O A or O B, the rotation should be in the same direction as regards the hands of a watch. These constructions are well known to all who have studied elementary mechanical principles. Obviously if the rotation about O A is very much greater than the rotation about O B, then the position of the new axis O C must be much nearer O A than O B.

We see then that if a body is spinning about an axis O A, and we apply forces to it which would, if it were at rest, turn it about the axis O B; the effect is to cause the spinning axis to be altered to O C; that

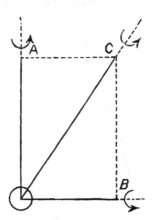

FIGURE 24

is, the spinning axis sets itself in better agreement with the new axis of rotation. This is the first statement on our wall sheet, the rule from which all our other statements are derived, assuming that they were not really derived from observation. Now I do not say that I have here given a complete proof for all cases, for the fly-wheels in these gyrostats are running in bearings, and the bearings constrain the axes to take the new positions, whereas there is no such constraint in this top; but in the limited time of a popular lecture like this it is not possible, even if it were desirable, to give an exhaustive proof of such a universal rule as ours is. That I have not exhausted all that might be said on this subject will be evident from what follows.

If we have a spinning ball and we give to it a new kind of rotation, what will happen? Suppose, for example, that the earth were a homogeneous sphere, and that there were suddenly impressed upon it a new rotatory motion tending to send Africa southwards; the axis of this new spin would have its pole at Java, and this new spin combined with the old one would cause the earth to have its true pole somewhere between the present pole and Java. It would no longer rotate about its present axis. In fact the axis of rotation would be altered, and there would be no tendency for anything further to occur, because a homogeneous sphere will as readily rotate about one axis as another. But if such a thing were to happen to this earth of ours, which is not

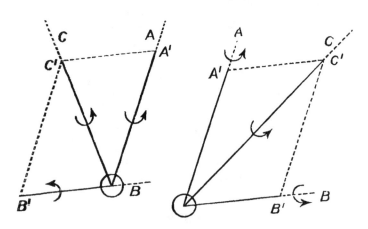

FIGURE 25

a sphere but a flattened spheroid like an orange, its polar diameter being the one-third of one per cent shorter than the equatorial diameter; then as soon as the new axis was established, the axis of symmetry would resent the change and would try to become again the axis of rotation, and a great wobbling motion would ensue. I put the matter in popular language when I speak of the resentment of an axis; perhaps it is better to explain more exactly what I mean. I am going to use the expression Centrifugal Force. Now there are captious critics who object to this term, but all engineers use it, and I like to use it, and our captious critics submit to all sorts of ignominious involution of language in evading the use of it. It means the force with which any body acts upon its constraints when it is constrained to move in a curved path. The force is always directed away from the centre of the curve. When a ball is whirled round in a curve at the end of a string its centrifugal force tends to break the string. When

FIGURE 26

any body keyed to a shaft is revolving with the shaft, it may be that the centrifugal forces of all the parts just balance one another; but sometimes they do not, and then we say that the shaft is out of balance. Here, for example, is a disc of wood rotating. It is in balance. But I stop its motion and fix this piece of lead, A, to it, and you observe when it rotates that it is so much out of balance that the bearings of the shaft and the frame that holds them, and even the lecture-table, are shaking. Now I will put things in balance again by placing another piece of lead, B, on the side of the spindle remote from A, and when I again rotate the disc (Fig. 26) there is no longer any shaking of the framework. When the crank-shaft of a locomotive has not been put in balance by means of weights suitably placed on the driving-wheels,

FIGURE 27

there is nobody in the train who does not feel the effects. Yes, and the coalbill shows the effects, for an unbalanced engine tugs the train spasmodically instead of exerting an efficient steady pull. My friend Professor Milne, of Japan, places earthquake measuring instruments on engines and in trains for measuring this and other wants of balance, and he has shown unmistakably that two engines of nearly the same general design, one balanced properly and the other not, consume very different amounts of coal in making the same journey at the same speed.

If a rotating body is in balance, not only does the axis of rotation pass through the centre of gravity (or rather centre of mass) of the body, but the axis of rotation must be one of the three principal axes through the centre of mass of the body. Here, for example, is an ellipsoid of wood; A A, B B, and C C (Fig. 27) are its three principal axes, and it would be in balance if it rotated about any one of these three axes, and it would not be in balance if it rotated about any other axis, unless, indeed, it were like a homogeneous sphere, every diameter of which is a principal axis.

Every body has three such principal axes through its centre of mass, and this body (Fig. 27) has them; but I have here constrained it to rotate about the axis D D, and you all observe the effect of the unbalanced centrifugal forces, which is nearly great enough to tear the framework in pieces. The higher the speed the more important this

GYROSCOPIC MOTION

want of balance is. If the speed is doubled, the centrifugal forces become four times as great; and modern mechanical engineers with their quick speed engines, some of which revolve. like the fan-engines of torpedo-boats, at 1700 revolutions per minute, require to pay great attention to this subject, which the older engineers never troubled their heads about. You must remember that even when want of balance does not actually fracture the framework of an engine, it will shake everything, so that nuts and keys and other fastenings are pretty sure to get loose.

I have seen, on a badly-balanced machine, a securely-fastened pair of nuts, one supposed to be locking the other, quietly revolving on their bolt at the same time, and gently lifting themselves at a regular but fairly rapid rate, until they both tumbled from the end of the bolt into my hand. If my hand had not been there, the bolts would have tumbled into a receptacle in which they would have produced interesting but most destructive phenomena. You would have somebody else lecturing to you to-night if that event had come off.

Suppose, then, that our earth were spinning about any other axis than its present axis, the axis of figure. If spun about any diameter of the equator for example, centrifugal forces would just keep things in a state of unstable equilibrium, and no great change might be produced until some accidental cause effected a slight alteration in the spinning axis, and after that the earth would wobble very greatly. How long and how violently it would wobble, would depend an a number of circumstances about which I will not now venture to guess. If you tell me that on the whole, in spite of the violence of the wobbling, it would not get shaken into a new form altogether, then I know that in consequence of tidal and other friction it would eventually come to a quiet state of spinning about its present axis.

You see, then, that although every body has three axes about which it will rotate in a balanced fashion without any tendency to wobble, this balance of centrifugal forces is really an unstable balance in two out of three cases, and there is only one axis about which a perfectly stable balanced kind of rotation will take place, and a spinning body generally comes to rotate about this axis in the long run if left to itself, and if there is friction to still the wobbling.

To illustrate this, I have here a method of spinning bodies which enables them to choose as their spinning axis that one principal axis about which their rotation is most stable. The various bodies can be hung at the end of this string, and I cause the pulley from which the string hangs to rotate. Observe that at first the disc (Fig. 28 *a*) rotates soberly about the axis A A, but you note the small beginning of the wobble; now it gets quite violent, and now the disc is stably and smoothly rotating about the axis B B, which is the most important of its principal axes.

Again, this cone (Fig. 28 *b*) rotates smoothly at first about the axis A A, but the wobble begins and gets very great, and eventually the cone rotates smoothly about the axis B B, which is the most important of its principal axes. Here again is a rod hung from one end (Fig. 28 *d*).

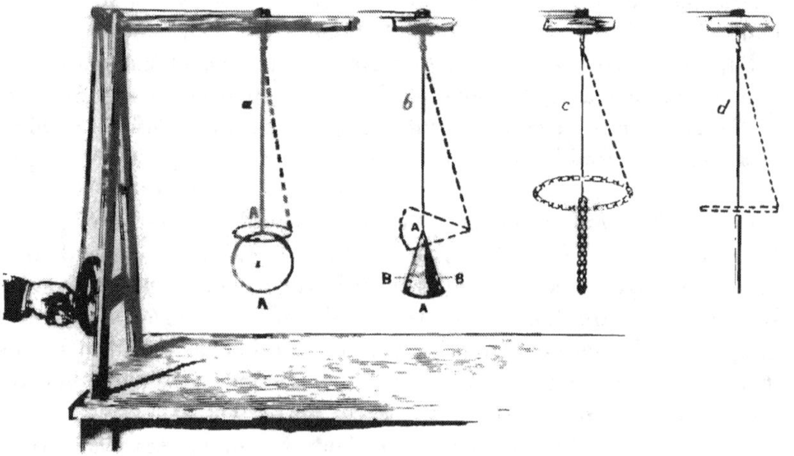
a
b
c
d
A
A
B
B
A
A

FIGURE 28

See also this anchor ring. But you may be more interested in this limp ring of chain (Fig. 28 *c*). See how at first it hangs from the cord vertically, and how the wobble and vibrations end in its becoming a perfectly circular ring lying all in a horizontal plane. This experiment illustrates also the quasi-rigidity given to a flexible body by rapid motion.

To return to this balanced gyrostat of ours (Fig. 13). It is not precessing, so you know that the weight W just balances the gyrostat F. Now if I leave the instrument to itself after I give a downward impulse to F, not exerting merely steady pressure, you will notice that F swings to the right for the reason already given; but it swings too fast and too far, just like any other swinging body, and it is easy from what I have already said, to see this wobbling motion (Fig. 29) should be the result, and that it should continue until friction stills it, and F takes its permanent new position only after some time elapses.

FIGURE 29

You see that I can impose this wobbling or nodding motion upon the gyrostat whether it has a motion of precession or not. It is now nodding as it precesses round and round—that is, it is rising and falling as it precesses.

Perhaps I had better put the matter a little more clearly. You see the same phenomenon in this top. If the top is precessing too fast for the force of gravity the top rises, and the precession diminishes in consequence; the precession being now too slow to balance gravity, the top falls a little and the precession increases again, and this sort of vibration about a mean position goes on just as the vibration of a pendulum goes on till friction destroys it, and the top precesses more regularly in the mean position. This nodding is more evident in the nearly horizontal balanced gyrostat than in a top, because in a top the turning effect of gravity is less in the higher positions.

When scientific men try to popularize their discoveries, for the sake of making some fact very plain they will often tell slight untruths, making statements which become rather misleading when their students reach the higher levels. Thus astronomers tell the public that the earth goes round the sun in an elliptic path, whereas the attractions of the planets cause the path to be only approximately elliptic; and electricians tell the public that electric energy is conveyed through wires, whereas it is really conveyed by all other space than that occupied by the wires. In this lecture I have to some small extent taken advantage of you in this way; for example, at first you will remember, I neglected the nodding or wobbling produced when an impulse is given to a top or gyrostat, and, all through, I neglect the fact that the instantaneous axis of rotation is only *nearly* coincident with the axis of figure of a precessing gyrostat or top. And indeed you may generally take it that if all one's statements were absolutely accurate, it would be necessary to use hundreds of technical terms and involved sentences with explanatory, police-like parentheses; and to listen to many such statements would be absolutely impossible, even for a scientific man. You would hardly expect, however, that so great a scientific man as the late Professor Rankine, when he was seized with the poetic fervour, would err even more than the popular lecturer in making his accuracy of statement subservient to the exigencies of the rhyme as well as to the necessity for simplicity of statement. He in his poem, *The Mathematician in Love*, has the following lines—

>"The lady loved dancing;—he therefore applied
>   To the polka and waltz, an equation;
>But when to rotate on his axis he tried,
>His centre of gravity swayed to one side,
>   And he fell by the earth's gravitation."

Now I have no doubt that this is as good "dropping into poetry" as can be expected in a scientific man, and ——'s science is as good as can be expected in a man who calls himself a poet; but in both cases we have illustrations of incompatibility of science and rhyming.

The motion of this gyrostat can be made even more complicated than it was when we had nutation and precession, but there is really nothing in it which is not readily explainable by the simple principles I have put before you. Look, for example, at this well-balanced gyrostat (Fig. 17). When I strike this inner gymbal ring in any way you

FIGURE 17

see that it wiggles quickly just as if it were a lump of jelly, its rapid vibrations dying away just like the rapid vibrations of any yielding elastic body. This strange elasticity is of very great interest when we consider it in relation to the molecular properties of matter. Here again (Fig. 30) we have an example which is even more interesting. I have supported the cased gyrostat of Figs. 5 and 6 upon a pair of stilts, and you will observe that it is moving about a perfectly stable position with a very curious staggering kind of vibratory motion; but there is nothing in these motions however curious, that you cannot easily explain if you have followed me so far.

Some of you who are more observant than the others, will have remarked that all these precessing gyrostats gradually fall lower and lower, just as they would do, only more quickly, if they were not spinning. And if you cast your eye upon the third statement of our wall sheet (p. 27) you will readily understand why it is so.

"Delay the precession and the body falls, as gravity would make it do if it were not spinning." Well, the precession of every one of these is resisted by friction, and so they fall lower and lower.

I wonder if any of you have followed me so well as to know already why a spinning top rises. Perhaps you have not yet had time to think it out, but I have accentuated several times the particular fact which explains this phenomenon. Friction makes the gyrostats fall, what is it that causes a top to rise? Rapid rising to the upright position is the invariable sign of rapid rotation in a top, and I recollect that when quite vertical we used to say, "She sleeps!" Such was the endearing way in which the youthful experimenter thought of the beautiful object of his tender regard.

All so well known as this rising tendency of a top has been ever since tops were first spun, I question, if any person in this hall knows the explanation, and I question its being known to more than a few persons anywhere. Any great mathematician will tell you that the explanation is surely to be found published in *Routh*, or that at all events he knows men at Cambridge who surely know it, and he thinks that he himself must have known it although he has now forgotten those elaborate mathematical demonstrations which he once exercised his mind upon. I believe that all such statements are made in error,

FIGURE 30

GYROSCOPIC MOTION

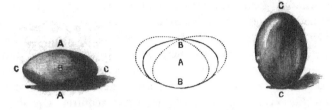

FIGURE 31

but I cannot be sure.[1] A partial theory of the phenomenon was given by Mr. Archibald Smith in the *Cambridge Mathematical Journal* many years ago, but the problem was solved by Sir William Thomson and Professor Blackburn when they stayed together one year at the seaside, reading for the great Cambridge mathematical examination. It must have alarmed a person interested in Thomson's success to notice that the seaside holiday was really spent by him and his friend in spinning all sorts of rounded stones which they picked up on the beach.

And I will now show you the curious phenomenon that puzzled him that year. This ellipsoid (Fig. 31) will represent a waterworn stone. It is lying in its most stable state on the table, and I give it a spin. You see that for a second or two it was inclined to go on spinning about the axis A A, but it began to wobble violently, and after a while, when these wobbles stilled, you saw that it was spinning nicely with its axis B B vertical; but then a new series of wobbling began and became more violent, and when they ceased you saw that the object had at length reached a settled state of spinning, standing upright upon its longest axis. This is an extraordinary phenomenon to any person who knows about the great inclination of this body to spin in the very way which I first started it spinning. You will find that nearly any rounded stone when spun will get up in this way upon its longest axis, if the spin is only vigorous enough, and in the very same way this spinning top tends to get more and more upright.

I believe that there are very few mathematical explanations of phenomena which may not be given in quite ordinary language to

[1] When this lecture containing the above statement was in the hands of the printers, I was directed by Prof. Fitzgerald to the late Prof. Jellet's *Treatise on the Theory of Friction*, published in 1872, and there at page 18 I found the mathematical explanation of the rising top.

people who have an ordinary amount of experience. In most cases the symbolical algebraic explanation must be given first by somebody, and then comes the time for its translation into ordinary language. This is the foundation of the new thing called Technical Education, which assumes that a workman may be taught the principles underlying the operations which go on in his trade, if we base our explanations on the experience which the man has acquired already, without tiring him with a four years' course of study in elementary things such as is most suitable for inexperienced children and youths at public schools and the universities.

With your present experience the explanation of the rising of the top becomes ridiculously simple. If you look at statement *two* on this wall sheet (p. 27) and reflect a little, some of you will be able, without any elaborate mathematics, to give the simple reason for this that Thomson gave me sixteen years ago. "Hurry on the precession, and the body rises in opposition to gravity." Well, as I am not touching the top, and as the body does rise, we look at once for something that is hurrying on the precession, and we naturally look to the way in which its peg is rubbing on the table, for, with the exception of the atmosphere this top is touching nothing else than the table. Observe carefully how any of these objects precesses. Fig. 32 shows the way in which a top spins. Looked at from above, if the top is spinning in the direction of the hands of a watch, we know from the fourth statement of our wall sheet, or by mere observation, that it also precesses in the direction of the hands of a watch; that is, its precession is such as to make the peg roll at B into the paper. For you will observe that the peg is rolling round a circular path on the table, G being nearly motionless, and the axis A G A describing nearly a cone in space whose vertex is G, above the table. Fig. 33 shows the peg enlarged, and it is evident that the point B touching the table is really like the bottom of a wheel B B', and as this wheel is rotating, the rotation causes it to roll *into* the paper, away from us. But observe its mere precession is making it roll *into* the paper, and that the spin if great enough wants to roll the top faster than the precession lets it roll, so that it hurries on the precession, and therefore the top rises. That is the simple explanation; the spin, so long as it is great enough,

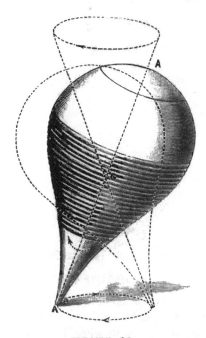

FIGURE 32

is always hurrying on the precession, and if you will cast your recollection back to the days of your youth, when a top was supported on your hand as this is now on mine (Fig. 34), and the spin had grown to be quite small, and was unable to keep the top upright, you will remember that you dexterously helped the precession by giving your hand a circling motion so as to get from your top the advantages as to uprightness of a slightly longer spin.

I must ask you now by observation, and the application of exactly the same argument, to explain the struggle for uprightness on its longer axis of any rounded stone when it spins on a table. I may tell you that some of these large rounded-looking objects which I now spin before you in illustration, are made hollow, and they are either of wood or zinc, because I have not the skill necessary to spin large objects, and yet I wanted to have objects which you would be able to see. This small one (Fig. 31) is the largest solid one to which my

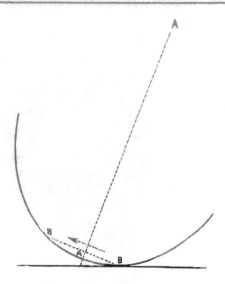

FIGURE 33

fingers are able to give sufficient spin. Here is a very interesting object (Fig. 35), spherical in shape, but its centre of gravity is not exactly at its centre of figure, so when I lay it on the table it always gets to its position of stable equilibrium, the white spot touching the table as at A. Some of you know that if this sphere is thrown into the air it seems to have very curious motions, because one is so apt to forget that it is the motion of its centre of gravity which

FIGURE 34

follows a simple path, and the boundary is eccentric to the centre of gravity. Its motions when set to roll upon a carpet are also extremely curious.

Now for the very reasons that I have already given, when this sphere is made to spin on the table, it always endeavours to get its white spot uppermost, as in C, Fig. 35; to get into the position in which when not spinning it would be unstable.

The precession of a top or gyrostat leads us at once to think of the precession of the great spinning body on which we live. You know that the earth spins on its axis a little more than once every twenty-

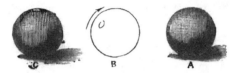

FIGURE 35

four hours, as this orange is revolving, and that it goes around the sun once in a year, as this orange is now going round a model sun, or as is shown in the diagram (Fig. 36). Its spinning axis points in the direction shown, very nearly to the star which is called the pole star, almost infinitely far away. In the figure and model I have exaggerated the elliptic nature of the earth's path, as is quite usual, although it may be a little misleading, because the earth's path is much more nearly circular than many people imagine. As a matter of fact the earth is about three million miles nearer the sun in winter than it is in summer. This seems at first paradoxical, but we get to understand it when we reflect that, because of the slope of the earth's axis to the ecliptic, we people who live in the northern hemisphere have the sun less vertically above us and have a shorter day in the winter, and hence each square foot of our part of the earth's surface receives much less heat every day, and so we feel colder. Now in about 13,000 years the earth will have precessed just half a revolution (*see* Fig. 38); the axis will then be sloped towards the sun when it is nearest, instead of away from it as it is now; consequently we shall be much warmer in summer and colder in winter than we are now. Indeed we shall then be much worse off than the southern hemisphere people are now, for they have plenty of oceanic water to temper their climate. It is easy to see the nature of the change from figures 36, 37, and 38, or from the model as I carry the orange and its symbolic knitting-needle round the model sun. Let us imagine an observer placed above this model, far above the north pole of the earth. He sees the earth rotating against the direction of the hands of a watch, and he finds that it precesses with the hands of a watch, so that spin and precession are in opposite directions. Indeed it is because of this that we have the word "precession," which we now apply to the motion of a top, although the precession of a top is in the same direction as that of the spin.

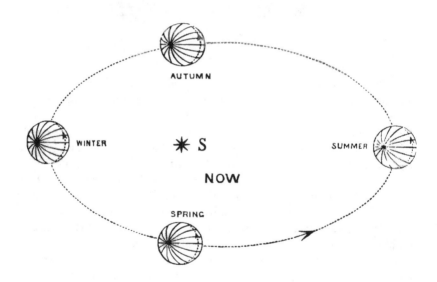

FIGURE 36

The practical astronomer, in explaining the *luni-solar precession of the equinoxes* to you, will not probably refer to tops or gyrostats. He will tell you that the *longitude* and *right ascension* of a star seem to alter; in fact that the point on the ecliptic from which he makes his measurements, namely, the spring equinox, is slowly travelling round the ecliptic in a direction opposite to that of the earth in its orbit, or

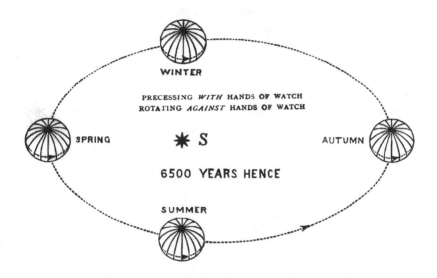

FIGURE 37

to the apparent path of the sun. The spring equinox is to him for heavenly measurements what the longitude of Greenwich is to the navigator. He will tell you that aberration of light, and parallax of the stars, but more than both, this precession of the equinoxes, are the three most important things which prevent us from seeing in an observatory by transit observations of the stars, that the earth is revolving with perfect uniformity. Both his way of describing the precession must not disguise for you the physical fact that his phenomenon and ours are identical, and that to us who are acquainted with spinning tops, the slow conical motion of a spinning axis is more readily understood than those details of his measurements in which an astronomer's mind is bound up, and which so often condemn a man of great intellectual power to the life of drudgery which we generally associate with the idea of the pound-a-week cheap clerk.

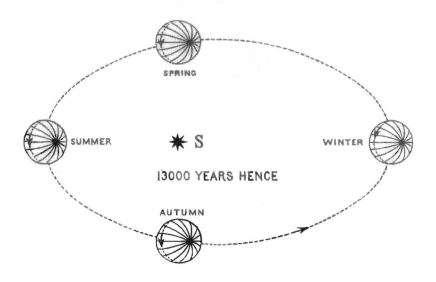

FIGURE 38

The precession of the earth is then of the same nature as that of a gyrostat suspended above its centre of gravity, of a body which would be stable and not top-heavy if it were not spinning. In fact the precession of the earth is of the same nature as that of this large gyrostat (Fig. 22), which is suspended in gymbals, so that it has a vibration like a pendulum when not spinning. I will now spin it, so that looked at from above it goes against the hands of a watch. Here again is a hemispherical wooden ship, in which there is a gyrostat with its axis vertical. It is in a stable equilibrium. When the gyrostat is not spinning, the ship vibrates slowly when put out of equilibrium; when the gyrostat is spinning the ship gets a motion of precession which is opposite in direction to that of the spinning. Astronomers, beginning

GYROSCOPIC MOTION

FIGURE 22

with Hipparchus, have made observations of the earth's motion for us, and we have observed the motions of gyrostats, and we naturally seek for an explanation of the precessional motion of the earth. The equator of the earth makes an angle of $23\frac{1}{2}°$ with the ecliptic, which is the plane of the earth's orbit. Or the spinning axis of the earth is always at the angle of $23\frac{1}{2}°$ with a perpendicular to the ecliptic, and makes a complete revolution in 26,000 years. The surface of the water on which this wooden ship is floating represents the ecliptic. The axis of spinning of the gyrostat is about $23\frac{1}{2}°$ to the vertical; the precession is in two minutes instead of 26,000 years; and only that this ship does not revolve in a great circular path, we should have in its precession a pretty exact illustration of the earth's precession.

The precessional motion of the ship, or of the gyrostat (Fig. 22), is explainable, and in the same way the earth's precession is at once explained if we find that there are forces from external bodies tending to put its spinning axis at right angles to the ecliptic. The earth is a nearly spherical body. If it were exactly spherical and homogeneous, the resultant force of attraction upon it, of a distant body, would be in a line through its centre. And again, if it were spherical and non-homogeneous, but if its mass were arranged in uniformly dense, spherical layers, like the coats of an onion. But the earth is not spherical, and to find what is the nature of the attraction of a distant body, it has been necessary to make pendulum observations all over the earth. You know that if a pendulum does not alter in length as we take it about to various places, its time of vibration at each place enables the force of gravity at each place to be determined; and Mr. Green proved that if we know the force of gravity at all places on the surface of the earth, although we may know nothing about the state of the inside of the earth, we can calculate with absolute accuracy the force exerted by the earth on matter placed anywhere outside the earth; for instance, at any part of the moon's orbit, or at the sun. And hence we know the equal and opposite force with which such matter will act on the earth. Now pendulum observations have been made at a great many places on the earth, and we know, although of course not with absolute accuracy, the attraction on the earth, of matter outside the earth. For instance, we know that the resultant attraction of the sun on the earth is a force which does not pass through the centre of the earth's mass. You may comprehend the result better if I refer to this diagram of the earth at midwinter (Fig. 39), and use a popular method of description. A and B may roughly be called the protuberant parts of the earth—that protuberant belt of matter which makes the earth orange-shaped instead of spherical. On the spherical portion inside, assumed roughly to be homogeneous, the resultant attraction is a force through the centre.

I will now consider the attraction on the protuberant equatorial belt indicated by A and B. The sun attracts a pound of matter at B more than it attracts a pound of matter at A, because B is nearer than A, and hence the total resultant force is in the direction M N rather than O O, through the centre of the earth's mass. But we know that a force O O parallel to M N, together with a tilting couple of forces tending to turn the equator edge on to the sun. You will get the true result as to the tilting tendency by imagining the earth to be motionless, and the sun's mass to be distributed as a circular ring of matter 184 millions of miles in diameter, inclined to the equator at $23\frac{1}{2}°$. Under the influence of the attraction of this ring the earth would heave like a great ship on a calm sea, rolling very slowly; in fact, making one complete swing in about three years. But the earth is spinning, and the tilting couple or torque acts upon it just like the forces which are always tending to cause this ship-model to stand upright, and hence it has a precessional motion whose complete period is 26,000 years. When there is no spin in the ship, its complete oscillation takes place in three

GYROSCOPIC MOTION

seconds, and when I spin the gyrostat on board the ship, the complete period of its precession is two minutes. In both cases the effect of the spin is to convert what would be an oscillation into a very much slower precession.

There is, however, a great difference between the earth and the gyrostat. The forces acting on the top are always the same, but the forces acting on the earth are continually altering. At midwinter and midsummer the tilting forces are greatest, and at the equinoxes in spring and autumn there are no such forces. So that the precessional motion changes its rate every quarter year from a maximum to nothing, or from nothing to a maximum. It is however, always in the same direction—the direction opposed to the earth's spin. When we speak then of the precessional motion of the earth, we usually think of the mean or average motion, since the motion gets quicker and slower every quarter year.

Further, the moon is like the sun in its action. It tries to tilt the equatorial part of the earth into the plane of the moon's orbit. The plane of the moon's orbit is nearly the same as that of the ecliptic, and hence the average precession of the earth is of much the same kind as if only one of the two, the moon or the sun, alone acted. That is, the general phenomenon of precession of the earth's axis in a conical

Further, the moon is like the sun in its action. It tries to tilt the sun and moon.

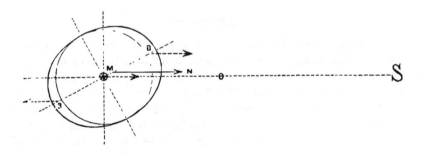

FIGURE 39

You will observe here an instance of the the sort of untruth which it is almost imperative to tell in explaining natural phenomena. Hitherto I had spoken only of the sun as producing precession of the earth. This was convenient, because the plane of the ecliptic makes always almost exactly $23\frac{1}{2}°$ with the earth's equator, and although on the whole the moon's action is nearly identical with that of the sun, and about twice as great, yet it varies considerably. The superior tilting action of the moon, just like its tide-producing action, is due to its being so much nearer us than the sun, and exists in spite of the very small mass of the moon as compared with that of the sun.

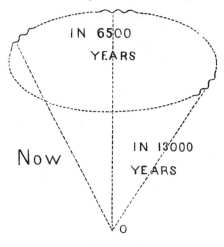

FIGURE 40

As the ecliptic makes an angle of $23\frac{1}{2}°$ with the earth's equator, and the moon's orbit makes an angle $5\frac{1}{2}°$ with the ecliptic, we see that the moon's orbit sometimes makes an angle of 29° with the earth's equator, and sometimes only 18°, changing from 29° to 18°, and back to 29° again in about nineteen years. This causes what is called "Nutation," or the nodding of the earth, for the tilting action due to the sun is greatly helped and greatly modified by it. The result of the variable nature of the moon's action is then that the earth's axis rotates in an elliptic conical path round what might be called its mean position. We have also to remember that twice in every lunar month the moon's tilting action on the earth is greater, and twice it is zero, and that it continually varies in value.

On the whole, then, the moon and sun, and to a small extent the planets, produce the general effect of a precession, which repeats itself in a period of about 25,695 years. It is not perfectly uniform, being performed at a speed which is a maximum in summer and winter; that is, there is a change of speed whose period is half a year; and there is a change of speed whose period is half a lunar month, the precession being quicker to-night than it will be next Saturday, when it will increase for about another week, and diminish the next. Besides this, because of $5\frac{1}{2}°$ of angularity of the orbits, we have something like the nodding of our precessing gyrostat, and the inclination of the earth's axis to the ecliptic is not constant at $23\frac{1}{2}°$, but is changing, its periodic time being nineteen years. Regarding, the earth's centre as fixed at O we see then, as illustrated in this model and in (Fig. 40), the axis of the earth describes almost a perfect circle on the celestial sphere once in 25,866 years, its speed fluctuating every half year and every half month. But it is not a perfect circle, it is really a wavy line, there being a complete wave nineteen years, and there are smalled ripples in it, corresponding to the half-yearly and fortnightly periods. But the very cause of the nutation, the nineteen-yearly period of retrogression of the moon's nodes, as it is called, is itself really produced as the precession of a gyrostat is produced, that is, by tilting forces acting on a spinning body.

Imagine the earth to be stationary, and the sun and moon revolving round it. It was Gauss who found that the present action is the same as if the masses of the moon and sun were distributed all round their orbits. For instance, imagine the moon's mass distributed over her orbit in the form of a rigid ring of 480,000 miles diameter, and imagine less of it to exist where the present speed is greater, so that the ring would be thicker at the moon's apogee, and thinner at the perigee. Such a ring round the earth would be similar to Saturn's rings, which have also a precession of nodes, only Saturn's rings are not rigid, else there would be no equilibrium. Now if we leave out of account the earth and imagine this ring to exist by itself, and that its centre simply had a motion round the sun in a year, since it makes an angle of $5\frac{1}{2}°$ with the ecliptic it would vibrate into the ecliptic till it made the same angle on the other side and back again. But it revolves once about its centre in twenty-seven solar days, eight hours, and it will no longer swing like a ship in a ground-swell, but will get a motion of precision opposed in direction to its own revolution. As the ring's motion is against the hands of a watch, looking from the north down on the ecliptic, this retrogression of the moon's nodes is in the direction of the hands of a watch. It is exactly the same sort of phenomenon as the precession of the equinoxes, only with a much shorter period of 6798 days instead of 25,866 years.

I told you how, if we knew the moon's mass or the sun's, we could tell the amount of the forces, or the torque as it is more properly called, with which it tries to tilt the earth. We know the rate at which the earth is spinning, and we have observed the precessional motion. Now when we follow up the method which I have sketched already, we find that the precessional velocity of a spinning body ought to be equal to the torque divided by spinning velocity and by the moment of inertia[1] of the body about the polar axis. Hence the greater the tilting forces, and the less the spin and the less the moment of inertia, the greater is the precessional speed. Given all of these elements except one, it is easy to calculate that unknown element. Usually what we aim at in such a calculation is the determination of the moon's mass, as this phenomenon of precession and the action of the tides are the only two natural phenomena which have yet enabled the moon's mass to be calculated.

I do not mean to apologize to you for the introduction of such terms as *Moment of Inertia*, nor do I mean to explain them. In this lecture I have avoided, as much as I could, the introduction of mathematical expressions and the use of technical terms. But I want you to understand that I am not afraid to introduce technical terms when giving a popular lecture. If there is any offence in such a practice, it must, in my opinion, be greatly aggravated by the addition of explanations of the precise meanings of such terms. The use of a correct technical term serves several useful purposes. First, it gives some satisfaction to the lecturer, as it enables him to state, very concisely, something which satisfies his

[1] Roughly, the *Inertia* or *Mass* of a body expresses its resistance to change of mere translational velocity, whereas, the *Moment of Inertia* of a body expresses its resistance to change of rotational velocity.

own weak inclination to have his reasoning complete, but which he luckily has not time to trouble his audience with. Second, it corrects the universal belief of all popular audiences that they know everything now that can be said on the subject. Third, it teaches everybody, including

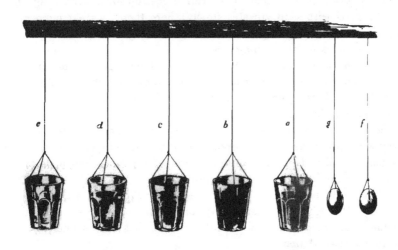

FIGURE 41

the lecturer, that there is nothing lost and often a great deal gained by the adoption of a casual method of skipping when one is working up a new subject.

Some years ago it was argued that if the earth were a shell filled with liquid, if this liquid were quite frictionless, then the moment of inertia of the shell is all that that we should have to take into account in considering precession, and that if it were viscous the precession would very soon disappear altogether. To illustrate the effect of the moment of inertia, I have hung up here a number of glasses—one a filled with sand, another b with treacle, a third c with oil, the fourth d with water, and the fifth e is empty (Fig. 41). You see that if I twist these suspending wires and release them, a vibratory motion is set up, just like that of the balance of a watch. Observe that the glass with water vibrates quickly, its effective moment of inertia being merely that of the glass itself, and you see that the time of swing is pretty much the same as that of the empty glass; that is, the water does not seem to move with the glass. Observe that the vibration goes on for a fairly long time.

The glass with sand vibrates slowly; here there is great moment of inertia, as the sand and glass behave like one rigid body, and again the vibration goes on for a long time.

In the oil and treacle, however, there are longer periods of vibration than in the case of the water or empty glass, and less than would be the case if the vibrating bodies were all rigid, but the vibrations are stilled more rapidly because of friction.

Boiled (f) and unboiled (g) eggs suspended from wires in the same way will exhibit the same differences in the behaviour of bodies, one of which is rigid and the other liquid inside; you see how much slower an oscillation the boiled has than the unboiled.

Even on the table here it is easy to show the difference between boiled and unboiled eggs. Roll them both; you see that one of them stops much sooner than the other; it is the unboiled one that stops sooner, because of its internal friction.

I must ask you to observe carefully the following very distinctive test of whether an egg is boiled or not. I roll the egg or spin it, and then place my finger on it just for an instant; long enough to stop the motion of the shell. You see that the boiled egg had quite finished its motion, but the unboiled egg's shell alone was stopped; the liquid inside goes on moving, and now renews the motion of the shell when I take my finger away.

It was argued that if the earth were fluid inside, the effective moment of inertia of the shell being comparatively small, and having, as we see in these examples, nothing whatever to do with the moment of inertia of the liquid, the precessional motion of the earth ought to be enormously quicker than it is. This was used as an argument against the idea of the earth's being fluid inside.

We know that the observed half-yearly and half-monthly changes of the precession of the earth would be much greater than they are if the

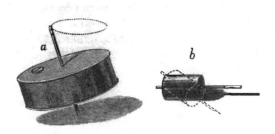

FIGURE 42

earth were a rigid shell containing much liquid, and if the shell were not nearly infinitely rigid the phenomena of the tides would not occur, but in regard to the general precession of the earth there is now no doubt that the old line of argument was wrong. Even if the earth were liquid inside, it spins so rapidly that it would behave like a rigid body in regard to such a slow phenomenon as precession of the equinoxes. In fact, in the older line of argument the important fact was lost sight of, that rapid rotation can give to even liquids a quasi-rigidity. Now here (Fig. 42 a) is a hollow brass top filled with water. The frame is light, and the water inside has much more mass than the outside frame, and if you test this carefully you will find that the top spins in almost exactly the same way as if the water were quite rigid; in fact, as if the whole top were rigid. Here you see it spinning and precessing just like any rigid top. This top, I know, is not filled with water, it is only partially filled; but whether partially or wholly filled it spins very much like a rigid top.

This is not the case with a long hollow brass top with water inside. I told you that all bodies have one axis about which they prefer to rotate. The outside metal part of a top behaves in a way that is now well known to you; the friction of its peg on the table compels it to get up on its longer axis. But the fluid inside a top is not constrained to spin on its longer axis of figure, and as it prefers its shorter axis like all these bodies I showed you, it spins in its own way, and by friction and pressure against the case constrains the case to spin about the shorter axis, annulling completely the tendency of the outside part to rise or keep up on its long axis. Hence it is found to be simply impossible to spin a long hollow top when filled with water.

Here, for example, is one (Fig. 42 b) that only differs from the last in being longer. It is filled, or partially filled, with water, and you observe that if I slowly get up a great spin when it is mounted in this frame, and I let it out on the table as I did the other one, this one lies down at once and refuses to spin on its peg. This difference of behaviour is most remarkable in two hollow tops you see before you (Fig.

FIGURE 43

43). They are both nearly spherical, both filled with water. They look so nearly alike that few persons among the audience are able to detect any difference in their shape. But one of them (a) is really slightly oblate like an orange, and the other (b) is slightly prolate like a lemon. I will give them both a gradually increasing rotation in this frame (Fig. 44) for a time sufficient to insure the rotation of the water inside. When just about to be set free to move like ordinary tops on the table, water and brass are moving like the parts of a rigid top. You see that the orange-shaped one continues to spin and precess, and gets itself upright when disturbed, like an ordinary rigid top; indeed I have seldom seen a better behaved top; whereas the lemon-shaped one lies down on its side at once, and quickly ceases to move in any way.

And now you will be able to appreciate a fourth test of a boiled egg, which is much more easily seen by a large audience than the last. Here is the unboiled one (Fig. 45 b). I try my best to spin it as it lies on the table, but you see that I cannot give it much spin, and so there is nothing of any importance to look at. But you observe that it is quite

GYROSCOPIC MOTION

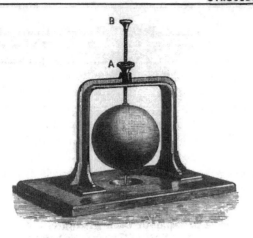

FIGURE 44

easy to spin the boiled egg, and that for reasons now well known to you it behaves like the stones that Thomson spun on the sea-beach; it gets up on its longer axis, a very pretty object for our educated eyes to look at (Fig. 45 *a*). You are all aware, from the behaviour of the lemon-shaped top, that even if, by the use of a whirling table suddenly stopped, or by any other contrivance, I could get up a spin in this unboiled egg, it would never make the slightest effort to rise on its end and spin about its longer axis.

I hope you don't think that I have been speaking too long about astronomical matters, for there is one other important thing connected

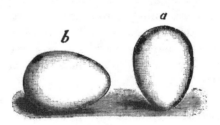

FIGURE 45

with astronomy that I must speak of. You see, I have had almost nothing practically to do with astronomy, and hence I have a strong interest in the subject. It is very curious, but quite true, that men practically engaged in any pursuit are almost unable to see the romance of it. This is what the imaginative outsider sees. But the overworked astronomer has a different point of view. As soon as it becomes one's duty to do a thing, and it is part of one's every-day work, the thing loses a great deal of its interest. We have been told by a great American philosopher that the only coachmen who ever saw the romance of coach-driving are those titled individuals who pay nowadays so largely for the privilege. In almost any branch of engineering you will find that if any invention is made it is the study of the subject with a fresh mind. Who ever heard of an old inhabitant of Japan or Peru writing an interesting book about those countries? At the end of two years' residence he sees only the most familiar things when he takes his walks abroad, and he feels unmitigated contempt for the ingenuous globe-trotter who writes a book about the country after a month's travel over the most beaten tracks in it. Now the experienced astronomer has forgotten the difficulties of his predecessors and the doubts of outsiders. It is a long time since he felt that awe in gazing at a starry sky and distances apart of the hosts of heaven. He speaks quite coolly of millions of years, and is nearly as callous when he refers to the ancient history of humanity on our planet as a weather-beaten geologist. The reason is obvious. Most of you know that the *Nautical Almanac* is as a literary production one of the most uninteresting works of reference in existence. It is even more disconnected than a dictionary, and I should think that preparing census-tables must be ever so much more romantic as an occupation than preparing the tables of the *Nautical Almanac*. And yet a particular figure, one of millions set down by an overworked calculator, may have all the tragic importance of life or death to the crew and passengers of a ship, when it is heading for safety or heading for the rocks under the mandate of that single printed character.

But this may not be a fair sort of criticism. I so seldom deal with astronomical matters, I know so little of the wear and tear and monotony of the every-day life of the astronomer, that I do not even know that the above facts are specially true about astronomers. I only know that they are very likely to be true because they are true of the other professional men.

I am happy to say that I come in contact with all sorts and conditions of men, and among others, with some men who deny many of the things taught in our earliest school-books. For example, that the earth is round, or that the earth revolves, or that Frenchmen speak a language different from ours. Now no man who has been to sea will deny the roundness of the earth, however greatly he may wonder at it; and no man who has been to France will deny that the French language is different from ours; but many men who learnt about the rotation of the earth in their school-days, and have had a plentiful opportunity of observing the heavenly bodies, deny the rotation of the earth. They tell you that the stars and moon are revolving about the earth, for they see them revolving night after night, and the sun revolves about the earth for they see it do so every day. And really if you think of it, it is not easy to prove the revolution of the earth. By the help of good telescopes and the electric telegraph or good chronometers, it is easy to show from the want of parallax in the stars that they must be very far away; but after all, we only know that either the earth revolves or else the sky revolves.[1] Of course, it seems infinitely more likely that the small earth should revolve than that the whole heavenly host should turn about the earth as a centre, and infinite likelihood is really absolute proof. Yet there is nobody who does not welcome an independent kind of proof. The phenomena of the tides, and nearly every new astronomical fact, may be said to be an addition to the proof. Still there is the absence of perfect certainty, and when we are told that these spinning-top phenomena give us a real proof of the rotation of the earth without our leaving the room, we welcome it, even although we may sneer at it as unnecessary after we have obtained it.

You know that a gyrostat suspended with perfect freedom about axes, which all pass through its centre of gravity, maintains a constant direction in space however its support may be carried. Its axis is not forced

[1] It is very unlikely, and certainly absurd-looking, hypothesis, but it seems that it is not contradicted by any fact in spectrum analysis, or even by any probable theory of the constitution of the interstellar ether, that the stars are merely images of our own sun, formed by reflections at the boundaries of the ether.

SPINNING TOPS

to alter its direction in any way. Now this gyrostat (Fig. 17) has not the perfect absence of friction at its axes of which I speak, and even the slightest friction will produce some constraint which is injurious to the experiment I am about to describe. It must be remembered, that if there were absolutely no constraint, then, even if the gyrostat were *not* spinning, its axis would keep a constant direction in space. But the spinning gyrostat shows its superiority in this, that any constraint due to friction is less powerful in altering the axis. The greater the spin, then, the better able are we to disregard effects due to friction. You have seen for yourselves the effect of carrying this gyrostat about in all sorts of ways—first, when it is not spinning and friction causes quite a large departure from constancy of direction of the axis; second, when it is spinning, and you see that although there is now the same friction as before, and I try to disturb the instrument more than before, the axis remains sensibly parallel to itself all the time. Now when this instrument is supported by the table it is really being carried around by the earth in its daily rotation. If the axis kept its direction perfectly, and it were now pointing horizontally due east, six hours after this it will point towards the north, but inclining downwards six hours afterwards it will point due west horizontally, and after one revolution of the earth it will

FIGURE 17

GYROSCOPIC MOTION

again point as it does now. Suppose I try the experiment, and I see that it points due east now in this room, and after a time it points due west, and yet I know that the gyrostat is constantly pointing in the same direction in space all the time, surely it is obvious that the room must be turning round in space. Suppose it points to the pole star now, in six hours, or twelve, or eighteen, or twenty-four, it will still point to the pole star.

Now it is not easy to obtain so frictionless a gyrostat that it will maintain a good spin for such a length of time as will enable the rotation of the room to be made visible to an audience. But I will describe to you how forty years ago it was proved in a laboratory that the earth turns on its axis. This experiment is usually connected with the name of Foucault, the same philosopher who with Fizeau showed how in a laboratory we can measure the velocity of light, and therefore measure the distance of the sun. It was suggested by Mr. Lang of Edinburgh in 1836, although only carried out in 1852 by Foucault. By these experiments, if you placed a body from which you could see no stars or other outside objects, say that you were living in underground regions, you could discover—first, whether there is a motion of rotation, and the amount of it; second, the meridian line or the direction of the true north; third, your latitude: Obtain a gyrostat like this (Fig. 46) but much larger, and far more frictionlessly suspended, so that it is free to move vertically or horizontally. For the vertical motion your gymbal pivots ought to be hard steel knife-edges. As for the horizontal freedom, Foucault used a fine steel wire. Let there be a fine scale engraved crosswise on the outer gymbal ring, and try to discover if it moves horizontally by means of a microscope with cross wires. When this is carefully done we find that there is a motion, but this is not the motion of the gyrostat, it is the motion of the microscope. In fact, the microscope and all other objects in the room are going round the gyrostat frame.

Now let us consider what occurs. The room is rotating about the earth's axis, and we know the rate of rotation; but we only want to know for our present purpose how much of the total rotation is about a vertical line in the room. If the room were at the North Pole, the whole rotation would be about the vertical line. If the room were at the equator, none of its rotation would be about a vertical line. In

FIGURE 46

our latitude now, the horizontal rate of rotation about a vertical axis is about four-fifths of the whole rate of rotation of the earth on its axis, and this is the amount that would be measured by our microscope. This experiment would give no result at a place on the equator, but in our latitude you would have a laboratory proof of the rotation of the earth. Foucault made the measurements with great accuracy.

If you now clamp the frame, and allow the spinning axis to have no motion except in a horizontal plane, the motion which the earth tends to give it about a vertical axis cannot now affect the gyrostat, but the earth constrains it to move about an axis due north and south, and consequently the spinning axis tries to put itself parallel to the north and south direction (Fig. 47). Hence with such an instrument it is easy to find the true north. If there were absolutely no friction the instrument would vibrate about the true north position like the compass needle (Fig. 50), although with an exceedingly slow swing.

It is with a curious mixture of feelings that one first recognizes the fact that all rotating bodies, fly-wheels of steam-engines and the like, are always tending to turn themselves towards the pole star; gently and vainly tugging at their foundations to get round towards the object of their adoration all the time they are in motion.

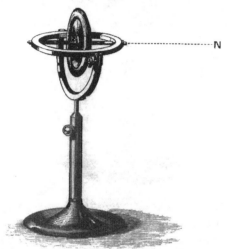

FIGURE 47

Now we have found the meridian as in (Fig. 47), we can begin a third experiment. Prevent motion horizontally, that is, about a vertical axis, but give the instrument freedom to move vertically in the meridian, like a transit instrument in an observatory about its horizontal axis. Its revolution with the earth will tend to make it change its angular position, and therefore it places itself parallel to the earth's axis; when in this position the daily rotation no longer causes any change in its direction in space, so it continues to point to the pole star (Fig. 48). It would be an interesting experiment to measure with a delicate chemical balance the force with which the axis raises itself, and in this way *weigh* the rotational motion of the earth.[1]

[1] Sir William Thomson has performed this.

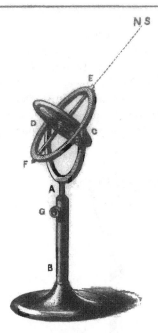

FIGURE 48

Now let us turn the frame of the instrument G B round a right angle, so that the spinning axis can only move in a plane at right angles to the meridian; obviously it is constrained by the vertical component of the earth's rotation, and points vertically downwards.

This last as well as the other phenomena of which I have spoken is very suggestive. Here is a magnetic needle (Fig. 49), sometimes called a dipping needle from the way in which it is suspended. If I turn its frame so that it can only move at right angles to the meridian, you see that it points vertically. You may reflect upon the analogous properties of this magnetic needle (Fig. 50) and of the gyrostat (Fig. 47); they both, when only capable of moving horizontally, point to the north; and you see that a very frictionless gyrostat might be used as a compass, or at all events as a corrector of compasses.[1] I have just put before you another analogy, and I want you to understand that, although

[1] It must be remembered that in one case I speak of the true north, and in the other of the magnetic north.

FIGURE 49

these are only analogies, they are not mere chance analogies, for there is undoubtedly a dynamical connection between the magnetic and the gyrostatic phenomena. Magnetism depends on the rotatory motion. The molecules of matter are in actual rotation, and a certain allineation of the axes of the rotations produces what we call magnetism. In steel bar not magnetized the little axes of rotation are all in different directions. The process of magnetization is simply bringing these rotations to be more or less round parallel axes, an allineation of the axes. A honeycombed mass with a spinning gyrostat in every cell, with all the spinning axes parallel, and the spins in the same direction, would—I was about to say, would be a magnet, but it would not be a magnet in all its properties, and yet it would resemble a magnet in many ways.[1]

[1] Rotating a large mass of iron rapidly in one direction and then in the other in the neighbourhood of a delicately-suspended magnetic needle, well protected from air currents, ought, I think, to give rise to magnetic phenomena of very great interest in the theory of magnetism. I have hitherto failed to obtain any trace of magnetic action, but I attribute my failure to the comparatively slow speed of rotation which I have employed, and to the want of delicacy of my magnetometer.

FIGURE 50

Some of you, seeing **electromotors** and other electric contrivances near this table, may think that they have to do with our theories and explanations of magnetic phenomena. But I must explain that this electromotor which I hold in my hand (Fig. 51) is used by me merely as the most convenient means I could find for the spinning of my tops and gyrostats. On the spindle of the motor is fastened a circular piece of wood; by touching this key I can supply the motor with electric energy, and the wooden disc is now rotating very rapidly. I have only to bring its rim in contact with any of these tops or gyrostats to set them spinning, and you see that I can set half a dozen gyrostats a-spinning in a few seconds; this chain of gyrostats, for instance. Again, this larger motor (Fig. 52), too large to move about in my hand, is fastened to the table, and I have used it to drive my larger contrivances; but you understand that I use these just as a barber might use them to

FIGURE 51

brush your hair, or Sarah Jane to clean the knives, or just as I would use a little steam-engine if it were more convenient for my purpose. It was more convenient for me to bring from London this battery of accumulators and these motors than to bring sacks of coals, and boilers, and steam-engines. But, indeed, all this has the deeper meaning that we can give to it if we like. Love is as old as the hills, and every day Love's messages are carried by the latest servant of man, the telegraph. These spinning tops were known probably to primeval man, and yet we have not learnt from them more than the most fractional portion of the lesson that they are always sending out to an unobservant world. Toys like these were spun probably by the builders of the Pyramids when they were boys, and here you see them side by side with the very latest of man's contrivances. I feel almost as Mr. Stanley might feel if, with the help of the electric light and a magic-lantern, he described his experiences in that dreadful African forest to the usual company of a London drawing-room.

The phenomena I have been describing to you play such a very important part in nature, that if time admitted I might go on expounding and explaining without finding any great reason to stop at one place rather than another. The time at my disposal allows me to refer to

FIGURE 52

only one other matter, namely, the connection between light and magnetism and the behaviour of spinning tops.

You are all aware that sound takes time to travel. This is a matter of common observation, as one can see a distant woodchopper lift his axe again before one hears the sound of his last stroke. A destructive sea wave is produced on the coast of Japan many hours after an earthquake occurs off the coast of America, the wave motion having taken time to travel across the Pacific. But although light travels more quickly than sound or wave motion in the sea, it does not travel with infinite rapidity, and the appearance of the eclipse of one of Jupiter's satellites is delayed by an observable number of minutes because light takes time to travel. The velocity has been measured by means of such observations, and we know that light travels at the rate of about 187,000 miles per second, or thirty thousand millions of centimetres per second. There is no doubt about this figure being nearly correct, for the velocity of light has been measured in the laboratory by a perfectly independent method.

Now the most interesting physical work done since Newton's time is the outcome of the experiments of Faraday and the theoretical deductions of Thomson and Maxwell. It is the theory that light and radiant heat are simply electro-magnetic disturbances propagated through space. I dare not do more than just refer to this matter, although it is of enormous importance. I can only say, that of all the observed facts in the sciences of light, electricity, and magnetism, we know of none that is in opposition to Maxwell's theory, and we know of many that support it. The greatest and earliest support that it had was this. If the theory is correct, then a certain electro-magnetic measurement ought to result in exactly the same quantity as the velocity of light. Now I want you to understand that the electric measurement is one of quantities that seem to have nothing whatever to do with light, except that one uses one's eyes in making the measurement; it requires the use of a two-foot rule and a magnetic needle, and coils of wire and currents of electricity. It seemed to bear a relationship to the velocity of light, which was not very unlike the fabled connection between Tenterden Steeple and the Goodwin Sands. It is a measurement which it is very difficult to make accurately. A number of skilful experimenters, working independently, and using quite different methods, arrived at results only one of which is as much as five per cent. different from the observed velocity of light, and some of them, on which the best dependence may be placed, agree exactly with the average value of the measurements of the velocity of light.

There is then a wonderful agreement of the two measurements, but without more explanation than I can give you now, you cannot perhaps understand the importance of this agreement between two seemingly unconnected magnitudes. At all events we now know, from the work of Professor Hertz in the last two years, that Maxwell's theory is correct, and that light is an electro-magnetic disturbance; and what is more, we know that electro-magnetic disturbances, incomparably slower than red-light or heat, are passing now through our bodies; that this now recognized kind of radiation may be reflected and refracted, and yet will pass through brick and stone walls and foggy atmospheres all military and marine and lighthouse signalling may be conducted in the future through the agency of this new and wonderful kind of radiation, of which what we call light is merely one form. Why at this moment, for all I know, two citizens of Leeds may be signalling to each other in this way through half a mile of houses, including this hall in which we are present.[1]

I mentioned this, the greatest modern philosophical discovery, because the germ of it, which was published by Thomson in 1856, makes direct reference to the analogy between the behaviour of our spinning-tops and magnetic and electrical phenomena. It will be easier, however, for us to consider here a mechanical illustration of the rotation of the plane of polarized light by magnetism which Thomson elaborated in 1874. This phenomenon may, I think, be regarded as the most important of all Faraday's discoveries. It was of enormous scientific importance, because it was not even suspected. Of his discovery of induced currents of electricty, to which all electric-lighting companies and transmission of power companies of the present day owe their being, Faraday himself said that it was a natural consequence of the discoveries of an earlier experimenter, Oersted. But this magneto-optic

[1] I had applied for a patent for this system of signalling some time before the above words were spoken, but although it was valid I allowed it to lapse in pure shame that I should have so unblushingly patented the use of the work of Fitzgerald and Hertz.

discovery was quite unexpected. I will now describe the phenomenon.

Some of you are aware that when a beam of light is sent through this implement, called a Nichol's Prism, it becomes polarized, or one-sided —that is, all the light that comes through is known to be propagated by vibrations which occur all in one plane. This rope (Fig. 53) hanging

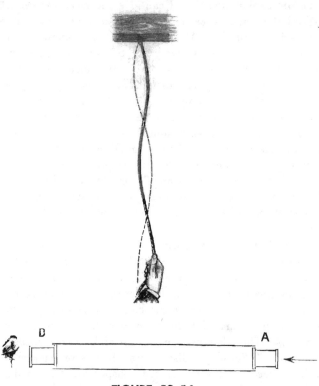

FIGURE 53-54

from the ceiling illustrates the nature of plane polarized light. All points in the rope are vibrating in the same plane. Well, this prism A, Fig. 54, only lets through it light that is polarized in a vertical plane. And Here at B I have a similar implement, and I place it so that it also will only allow light to pass through it which is polarized in a vertical plane. Hence most of the light coming through the polarizer, as the first prism is called, will pass readily through the analyzer, as the second is called, and I am now letting this light enter my eye. But when I turn the analyzer round through a right angle, I find that I see no light; there was a gradual darkening as I rotated the analyzer. The analyzer will now only allow light to pass through which is polarized in a horizontal plane, and it receives no such light.

You will see in this model (Fig. 55) a good illustration of polarized light. The white, brilliantly illuminated thread M N is pulled by a weight beyond the pulley M, and its end N is fastened to one limb of a tuning-fork. Some ragged-looking pieces of thread round the portion

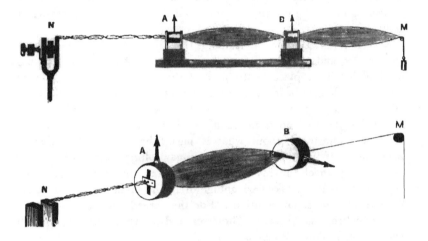

FIGURE 55

N A prevent its vibrating in any very determinate way, but from A to M the thread is free from all encumbrance. A vertical slot at A, through which the thread passes, determines the nature of the vibration of the part A B; every part of the thread between A and B is vibrating in up and down directions only. A vertical slot in B allows the vertical vibration to be communicated through it, and so we see the part B M vibrating in the same way as A B. I might point out quite a lot of ways in which this is not a perfect illustration of what occurs with light in Fig. 54. But it is quite good enough for my present purpose. A is a polarizer of vibration; it only allows up and down motion to pass through it, and B also allows up and down motion to pass through. But now, as B is turned round, it lets less and less of the up and down motion pass through it, until when it is in the second position shown in the lower part of the figure, it allows no up and down motion to pass through, and there is no visible motion of the thread between B and M. You will observe that if we did not know in what plane (in the present case the plane is vertical) the vibrations of the thread between A and B occurred, we should only have to turn B round until we found no vibration passing through, to obtain the information. Hence, as in the light case, we may call A a polarizer of vibrations, and B an analyzer.

Now if polarized light is passing from A to B (Fig 54) through the air, say, and we have the analyzer placed so that there is darkness, we find that if we place in the path of the ray some solution of sugar we shall no longer have darkness at B; we must turn B round to get things dark again; this is evidence of the sugar solution having twisted round the plane of polarization of the light. I will now assume that you know something about what is meant by twisting the plane of polarization of light. You know that sugar solution will do it, and the longer the path of the ray through the sugar, the more twist is gets. This phenomenon is taken advantage of in the sugar industries, to find the strengths of sugar solutions. For the thread illustration I am indebted to Professor Silvanus Thomson, and the next piece of apparatus which I shall show also belongs to him.

I have here (Fig. 55 *a*) a powerful armour-clad coil, or electromagnet. There is a central hole through it, through which a beam of light may be passed from an electric lamp, and I have a piece of Faraday's heavy glass nearly filling this hole. I have a polarizer at one end, and an analyzer at the other. You see now that the polarized light passes through the heavy glass and the analyzer, and enters the eye of an observer. I will now turn B until the light no longer passes. Until now there has been no magnetism, but I have the means here of producing a most intense magnetic field in the direction in which the ray passes, and if your eye were here you would see that there

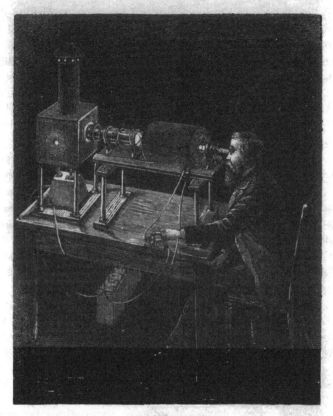

FIGURE 55A

is light passing through the analyzer. The magnetism has done something to the light, it has made it capable of passing where it could not pass before. When I turn the analyzer a little I stop the light again, and I know that what the magnetism did was to convert the glass into a medium like the sugar, a medium which rotates the plane of polarization of light.

In this experiment you have had to rely upon my personal measurement of the actual rotation produced. But if I insert between the polarizer and analyzer this disc of Professor Silvanus Thomson's, built of twenty-four radial pieces of mica, I shall have a means of showing to this audience the actual rotation of the plane of polarization of light. You see now on the screen the light which has passed through the analyzer in the form of a cross, and if the cross rotates it is a sign of the rotation of the plane of polarization of the light. By means of this electric key I can create, destroy, and reverse the magnetic field in the glass. As I create magnetism you see the twisting of the cross; I destroy the magnetism, and it returns to its old position; I create the opposite kind of magnetism, and you see that the cross twists in the opposite way. I hope it is now known to you that magnetism rotates the plane of polarization of light as the solution of sugar did.

As an illustration of what occurs between polarizer and analyzer, look again at this rope (Fig. 53) fastened to the ceiling. I move the bottom end sharply from east to west, and you see that every part of the rope moves from east to west. Can you imagine a rope such that when the bottom end was moved from east to west, a point some yards up moved from east-north-east to west-south-west, that a higher point moved from north-east to south-west, and so on, the direction gradually changing for higher and higher points? Some of you, knowing what I have done, may be able to imagine it. We should have what we want if this rope were a chain of gyrostats such as you see figured in the diagram; gyrostats all spinning in the same way looked at from below, with frictionless hinges between them. Here is such a chain (Fig. 56), one of many that I have tried to use in this way for several years. But although I have often believed that I saw the phenomenon occur in such a chain, I must now confess to repeated failures. The difficulties I have met with are almost altogether mechanical ones. You see that by touching all the gyrostats in succession with this rapidly revolving disc driven by the little electro-motor, I can get them all to spin at the same time; but you will notice that what with bad mechanism and bad calculation on my part, and want of skill, the phenomenon is completely masked by wild movements of the gyrostats, the causes of which are better known than capable of rectification. The principle of the action is very visible in this gyrostat suspended as the bob of a pendulum (Fig. 57). You may imagine this to represent a particle of the substance which transmits light in the magnetic field, and you see by the trickling thin stream of sand which falls from

GYROSCOPIC MOTION

it on the paper that it is continually changing the plane of polarization. But I am happy to say that I can show you to-night a really successful illustration of Thomson's principle; it is the very first time that this most suggestive experiment has been shown to an audience. I have a number of double gyrostats (Fig. 58) placed on the same line, joined

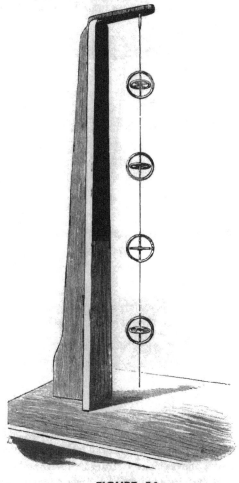

FIGURE 56

end to end by short pieces of elastic. Each instrument is supported at its centre of gravity, and it can rotate both in horizontal and in vertical planes.

The end of the vibrating lever A can only get a horizontal motion from my hand, and the motion is transmitted from one gyrostat to the next, until it has travelled to the very end one. Observe that when the gyrostats are not spinning, the motion is everywhere hori-

FIGURE 57

zontal. Now it is very important not to have any illustration here of a reflected ray of light, and so I have introduced a good deal of friction at all the supports. I will now spin all the gyrostats, and you will observe that when A moves nearly straight horizontally, the next gyrostat moves straight but in a slightly different plane, the second gyrostat moves in another plane, and so on, each gyrostat slightly twisting the plane in which the motion occurs; and you see that the end one does not by any means receive the horizontal motion of A, but a motion nearly vertical. This is a mechanical illustration, the first successful one I have made after many trials, of the effect on light of magnetism. The reason for the action that occurs in this model must be known to everybody who has tried to follow me from the beginning of the lecture.

And you can all see that we have only to imagine that many particles of the glass are rotating like gyrostats, and that magnetism has partially caused an allineation of their axes to have a dynamical theory of Faraday's discovery. The magnet twists the plane of polarization, and so does the solution of sugar; but it is found by experiment that the magnet does it indifferently for coming and going, whereas the sugar

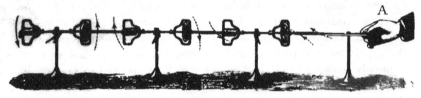

FIGURE 58

does it in a way that corresponds with a spiral structure of molecules. You see that in this important particular the gyrostat analogue must follow the magnetic method, and not the sugar method. We must regard this model, then, the analogue to Faraday's experiment, as giving great support to the idea that magnetism consists of rotation.

I have already exceeded the limits of time usually allowed to a popular lecturer, but you see that I am very far from having exhausted our subject. I am not quite sure that I have accomplished the object with which I set out. My object was, starting from the very different behaviour of a top when spinning and when not spinning, to show you that the observation of that very common phenomenon, and a determination to understand it, might lead us to understand very much more complex-looking things. There is no lesson which is more important to learn than this—That it is in the study of every-day facts that all the great discoveries of the future lie. Three thousand years ago spinning tops were common, but people never studied them. Three thousand years ago people boiled water and made steam, but the steam-engine was unknown to them. They had charcoal and saltpetre and sulphur, but they knew nothing of gunpowder. They saw fossils in rocks, but the wonders of geology were unstudied by them. They had bits of iron and copper, but not one of them thought of any one of the fifty simple ways that are now known to us of combining those known things into a telephone. Why, even the simplest kind of signalling by flags or lanterns was unknown to them, and yet a knowledge of this might have changed the fate of the world on one of the great days of battle that we read about. We look on Nature now in an utterly different way, with a great deal more reverence, and with much less unreasoning superstitious fear. And what we are to the people of three thousand years ago, so will be the people of one hundred years hence to us; for indeed the acceleration of the rate of progress in science is itself accelerating. The army of scientific workers gets larger and larger every day, and it is my belief that every unit of the population will be a scientific worker before long. And so we are gradually making time and space yield to us and obey us. But just think of it! Of all the discoveries of the next hundred years; the things that are unknown to us, but which will be so well known to our descendants that they will sneer at us as utterly ignorant, because these things will seem to them such self-evident facts; I say, of all these things, if one of us to-morrow discovered one of them, he would be regarded as a great discoverer. And yet the children of a hundred years hence will know it: it will be brought home to them perhaps at every footfall, at the flapping of every coat-tail.

Imagine the following question set in a school examination paper of 2090 A.D.—"Can you account for the crass ignorance of our forefathers in not being able to see from England what their friends were doing in Australia?"[1] Or this—"Messages are being received every minute from our friends on the planet Mars, and are now being an-

[1] How to see by electricity is perfectly well known, but no rich man seems willing to sacrifice the few thousands of pounds which are necessary for making the apparatus. If I could spare the money and time I would spend them in doing this thing—that is, I think so—but it is just possible that if I could afford to throw away three thousand pounds, I might feel greater pleasure in the growth of a great fortune than in any other natural process.

swered: how do you account for our ancestors being utterly ignorant that these messages were occasionally sent to them?" Or this—"What metal is as strong compared with steel as steel is compared with lead? and explain why the discovery of it was not made in Sheffield."

But there is one question that our descendants will never ask in accents of jocularity, for to their bitter sorrow every man, woman, and child of them will know the answer, and that question is this—"If our ancestors in the matter of coal economy were not quite as ignorant as a baby who takes a penny as equivalent for a half-crown, why did they waste our coal? Why did they destroy what never can be replaced?"

My friends, let me conclude by impressing upon you the value of knowledge, and the importance of using every opportunity within your reach to increase your own store of it. Many are the glittering things that seem to compete successfully with it, and to exercise a stronger fascination over human hearts. Wealth and rank, fashion and luxury, power and fame—these fire the ambitions of men, and attract myriads of eager worshippers; but, believe it, they are but poor things in comparison with knowledge, and have no such pure satisfactions to give as those which it is able to bestow. There is no evil thing under the sun which knowledge, when wielded by an earnest and rightly directed will, may not help to purge out and destroy; and there is no man or woman born into this world who has not been given the capacity, not merely to gather in knowledge for his own improvement and delight, but even to add something, however little, to that general stock of knowledge which is the world's best wealth.

NOTE, page 19, line 8.—Sir G. Greenhill's investigations show that the projectile precesses about the tangent to the path. Air friction stills the precession and causes the axis to get nearer the tangential direction. The ratio of length of projectile to diameter is very important for stability.

ARGUMENT

ARGUMENT

1. *Introduction*, pages 1—4, showing the importance of the study of spinning-top behaviour.
2. *Quasi-rigidity induced even in flexible and fluid bodies by rapid motion*, 4—9.
    Illustrations: Top, 4; belt or rope, 5; disc of thin paper, 5; ring of chain, 6; soft hat, 6; drunken man, 6; rotating water, 7; smoke rings 7; Thomson's Molecular Theory, 8; swimmer caught in an eddy, 8; mining water jet, 8; cased gyrostat, 8.
3. *The nature of this quasi-rigidity in spinning bodies is a resistance to change of direction of the axis of spinning*, 9—14.
    Illustrations: Cased gyrostat, 8—11; tops, biscuits, hats, thrown into the air, 11—12; quoits, hoops, projectiles from guns, 12; jugglers at the Victoria Music Hall, 13—14; child trundling hoop, man on bicycle, ballet-dancer, the earth pointing to pole star, boy's top, 14.
4. *Study of the crab-like behaviour of a spinning body*, 15—27.
    Illustrations: Spinning top, 15; cased gyrostat, 16; balanced gyrostat, 16—18; windage of projectiles from rifled guns, 18—19; tilting a hoop or bicycle, turning quickly on horseback, 19; bowls, 20; how to simplify one's observations, 20, 21; the illustration which gives us our simple universal rule, 21—22; testing the rule, 22—24; explanation of precession of gyrostat, 24, 25; precession of common top, 25; precession of overhung top, 25; list of our results given in a wall sheet, 26, 27.
5. *Proof or explanation of our simple universal rule*, 27—30.
    Giving two independent rotations to a body, 28, 29; composition of rotations, 29, 30.
6. *Warning that the rule is not, after all, so simple*, 30—37.
    Two independent spins given to the earth, 30; centrifugal force, 31; balancing of quick speed machinery, 31, 32; the possible wobbling of the earth, 33; the three principal axes of a body, 33; the free spinning of discs, cones, rods, rings of chain, 34; nodding motion of a gyrostat, 35; of a top, 35; parenthesis about inaccuracy of statement and Rankine's rhyme, 36, 37; further complications in gyrostatic behaviour, 37; strange elastic, jelly-like behaviour, 37; gyrostat on stilts, 37.

7. *Why a gyrostat falls*, 37, 38.
8. *Why a top rises*, 38—43.

    General ignorance, 38; Thomson preparing for the mathematical tripos, 39; behaviour of a water-worn stone when spun on a table, 39, 40; parenthesis on technical education, 40; simple explanation of why a top rises, 40—43; behaviour of heterogeneous sphere when spun, 42, 43.

9. *Precessional motion of the earth*, 43—53.

    Its nature and effects on climate, 43—46; resemblance of the precessing earth to certain models, 46, 47; tilting forces exerted by the sun and moon on the earth, 47, 48; how the earth's precessional motion is always altering, 49—51, the retrogression of the moon's nodes is itself another example, 51, 52; an exact statement made and a sort of apology for making it, 52, 53.

10. *Influence of possible internal fluidity of the earth on its precessional motion*, 53—57.

    Effects of fluids and sand in tumblers, 53, 54; three tests of the internal rigidity of an egg, that is, of its being a boiled egg, 54; quasi-rigidity of fluids due to rapid motion, forgotten in original argument, 55; beautiful behaviour of hollow top filled with water, 55; striking contrasts in the behaviour of two tops which are very much alike, 55, 56; fourth test of a boiled egg, 56, 57.

11. Apology for dwelling further upon astronomical matters, and impertinent remarks about astronomers, 57, 58.

12. How a gyrostat would enable a person living in subterranean regions to know, 1st, *that the earth rotates*; 2nd, *the amount of rotation*; 3rd, *the direction of true north*; 4th, *the latitude*, 59—65.

    Some men's want of faith, 59; disbelief in the earth's rotation, 59; how a free gyrostat behaves, 59—61; Foucault's laboratory measurement of the earth's rotation, 61, 62; to find the true north, 62; all rotating bodies vainly endeavouring to point to the pole star, 63; to find the latitude, 64; needle, 64, 65; dynamical connection between magnetism and gyrostatic phenomena, 65.

13. How the lecturer spun his tops, using electro-motors, 65—67.

14. *Light, magnetism, and molecular spinning tops*, 67—77.

    Light takes time to travel, 68; the electro-magnetic theory of light, 68, 69; signalling through fogs and buildings by means of a new kind of radiation, 69; Faraday's rotation of the plane of polarization by magnetism, with illustrations and models, 69—74; chain of gyrostats, 74; gyrostat as a pendulum bob, 74; Thomson's mechanical illustration of Faraday's experiment, 75—77.

15. *Conclusion*, 77—79.

    The necessity for cultivating the observation, 77; future discovery, 77; questions to be asked one hundred years hence, 78; knowledge the thing most to be wished for, 79.

APPENDIX #1

BRENNAN'S MONO-RAIL MODEL

APPENDIX #1

THE USE OF GYROSTATS

IN 1874 two famous men made a great mistake in endeavouring to prevent or diminish the rolling motion of the saloon of a vessel by using a rapidly rotating wheel. Mr. Macfarlane Gray pointed out their mistake. It is only when the wheel is allowed to *precess* that it can exercise a steadying effect; the moment which it then exerts is equal to the angular speed of the precession multiplied by the moment of momentum of the spinning wheel.

It is astonishing how many engineers who know the laws of motion of mere translation, are ignorant of angular motion, and yet the analogies between the two sets of laws are perfectly simple. I have set out these analogies in my book on *Applied Mechanics*. The last of them between centripetal force on a body moving in a curved path, and torque or moment on a rotating body is the simple key to all gyrostatic or top calculation. When the spin of a top is greatly reduced it is necessary to remember that the total moment of momentum is not about the spinning axis (see my *Applied Mechanics*, page 594); correction for this is, I suppose, what introduces the complexity which scares students from studying the vagaries of tops; but in all cases that are likely to come before an engineer it would be absurd to study such a small correction, and consequently calculation is exceedingly simple.

Inventors using gyrostats have succeeded in doing the following things—

(1) Keeping the platform of a gun level on board ship, however the ship may roll or pitch. Keeping a submarine vessel or a flying machine with any plane exactly horizontal or inclined in any specified

way.[1] It is easy to effect such objects without the use of a gyrostat, as by means of spirit levels it is possible to command powerful electric or other motors to keep anything always level. The actual methods employed by Mr. Beauchamp Tower (an hydraulic method), and by myself (an electric method), depend upon the use of a gyrostat, which is really a pendulum, the axis being vertical.

(2) Greatly reducing the rolling (or pitching) of a ship, or the saloon of a ship. This is the problem which Mr. Schlick has solved with great success, at any rate in the case of torpedo boats.

(3) In Mr. Brennan's Mono-rail railway, keeping the resultant force due to weight, wind pressure, centrifugal force, etc., exactly in line with the rail, so that, however the load on a wagon may alter in position, and although the wagon may be going round a curve, it is quickly brought to a position such that there are no forces tending to alter its angular position. The wagon leans over towards the wind or towards the centre of the curve of the rail so as to be in equilibrium.

(4) I need not refer to such matters as the use of gyrostats for the correction of compasses on board ship, referred to in page 64.

Problems (2) and (3) are those to which I wish to refer. For a ship of 6,000 tons Mr. Schlick would use a large wheel of 10 to 20 tons, revolving about an axis E F (fig. 1) whose mean position is vertical. Its bearings are in a frame E C F D which can move about a thwart-ship axis C D with a precessional motion. Its centre of gravity is below this axis, so that like a ship itself the frame is in stable equilibrium. Let the ship have rolled through an angle R from its upright position, and suppose the axis E F to have precessed through the angle P from a vertical position. Let the angular velocity of rolling be called R, and the angular velocity of precession P; let the moment of momentum of the wheel be m. For any vibrating body like a ship it is easy to write out the equation of motion; into this equation we have merely to introduce the moment m P diminishing R; into the equation for P we merely introduce the moment m R increasing P. As usual we introduce frictional terms; in the first place F R (F being a constant co-efficient) stilling the roll of the ship; in the second case f P a fluid friction introduced by a pair of dash pots applied at the pins. A and B

[1] Probably first described by Mr. Brennan.

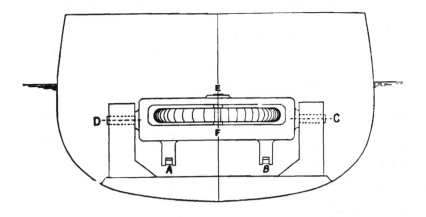

FIGURE 1

to still the precessional vibrations of the frame. It will be found that the angular motion P is very much greater than the roll R. Indeed, so great is P that there are stops to prevent its exceeding a certain amount. Of course so long as a stop acts, preventing precession, the roll of the ship proceeds as if the gyrostat wheel were not rotating. Mr. Schlick drives his wheels by steam; he will probably in future do as Mr. Brennan does, drive them by electromotors, and keep them in air-tight cases in good vacuums, because the loss of energy by friction against an atmosphere is proportional to the density of the atmosphere. The solution of the equations to find the nature of the R and P motions is sometimes tedious, but requires no great amount of mathematical knowledge. In a case considered by me of a 6,000 ton ship, the period of roll was increased from 14 to 20 seconds by the use of the gyrostat, and the roll rapidly diminished in amount. There was accompanying this slow periodic motion, one of a two seconds' period, but if it did appear it was damped out with great rapidity. Of course it is assumed that, by the use of bilge keels and rolling chambers, and as low a metacentre as is allowable, we have already lengthened the time of vibration, and damped the roll R as much as possible, before applying the gyrostat. I take it that everybody knows the importance of lengthening the period of the natural roll of a ship, although he may not know the reason. The reason why modern ships of great tonnage are so steady is because their natural periodic times of rolling vibration are so much greater than the probable periods of any waves acts upon a ship tending to make it roll, if the periodic time of each wave is not very different from the natural periodic time of vibration of the ship, the rolling motion may become dangerously great.

If we try to apply Mr. Schlick's method to Mr. Brennan's car it is easy to show that there is instability of motion, whether there is or is not friction. If there is no friction, and we make the gyrostat frame unstable by keeping its centre of gravity above the axis C D, there will be vibrations, but the smallest amount of friction will cause these vibrations to get greater and greater. Even without friction there will be instability if m, the moment of momentum of the wheel, is less than a certain amount. We see, then, that no form of the Schlick method, or modification of it, can be applied to solve the Brennan problem.

Mr. Brennan's method of working is quite different from that of Mr. Schlick. Illustration p. 86 shows his model car (about six ft. long); it is driven by electric accumulators carried by the car. His gyrostat wheels are driven by electromotors (not shown in fig. 2); as they are revolving in nearly vacuous spaces they consume but little power, and even if the current were stopped they would continue running at sufficiently high speeds to be effective for a length of time. Still it must not be forgotten that energy is wasted in friction, and work has to be done in bringing the car to a new position of equilibrium, and this energy is supplied by the electromotors. Should the gyrostats really stop, or fall to a certain low speed, two supports are automatically dropped, one on either side of the car; each of them drops till it reaches the ground; one of them dropping, perhaps, much farther than the other.

The real full-size car, which he is now constructing, may be pulled with other cars by any kind of locomotive using electricity or petrol or steam, or each of the wheels may be a driving wheel. He would prefer to generate electro-power on his train, and to drive every wheel with an electric motor. His wheels are so independent of one another that they can take very quick curves and vertical inequalities of the rail. The rail is fastened to sleepers lying on ground that may have sidelong slope. The model car is supported by a mono-rail bogie at each end; each

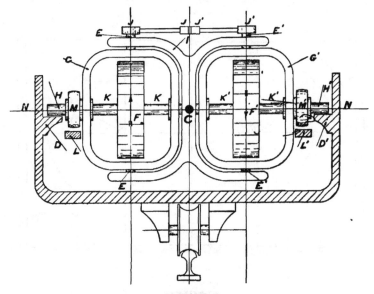

FIGURE 2

bogie has two wheels pivoted both vertically and horizontally; it runs on a round iron gas pipe, and sometimes on steel wire rope; the ground is nowhere levelled or cut, and at one place the rail is a steel wire rope spanning a gorge, as shown in illustration p.86. It is interesting to stop the car in the middle of this rope and to swing the rope sideways to see the automatic balancing of the car. The car may be left here or elsewhere balancing itself with nobody in charge of it. If the load on the car—great lead weights—be dumped about into new positions, the car adjusts itself to the new conditions with great quickness. When the car is stopped, if a person standing on the ground pushes the car sidewise, the car of course pushes in opposition, like an indignant animal, and by judicious pushing and yielding it is possible to cause a considerable tilt. Left now to itself the car rights itself very quickly.

Fig. 2 is a diagrammatic representation of Mr. Brennan's pair of gyrostats in sectional elevation and plan. The cases G and G', inside which the wheels F and F' are rotating *in vacuo* at the same speed and in opposite directions (driven by electromotors not shown in the

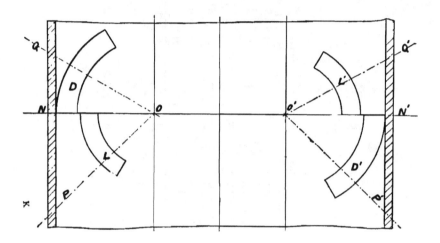

FIGURE 3

figure), are pivoted about vertical axes E J and E' J'. They are connected by spur-toothed segments J J and J' J', so that their precessional motions are equal and opposite. The whole system is pivoted about C, a longitudinal axis. Thus when precessing so that H comes out of the paper, so will H', and when H goes into the paper, so does H'. When the car is in equilibrium the axes K H and K' H' are in line N O O' N' across the car in the plane of the paper. They are also in a line which is at right angles to the total resultant (vertical or nearly vertical) force on the car. I will call N O O' N' the mid position. Let $\frac{1}{2}m$ be the moment of momentum of either wheel. Let us suppose that suddenly the car finds that it is not in equilibrium because of a gust of wind, or centrifugal force, or an alteration of loading, so that the shelf D comes up against H, the spinning axis (or a roller revolving with the spinning axis) of the gyrostat. H begins to roll away from me, and if no slipping occurred (but there always is slipping, and indeed, slipping is a necessary condition) it would roll, that is, the gyrostats would precess with a constant angular velocity a, and exert the moment ma upon the shelf D, and therefore on the car. It is to be observed that this is greater as the diameter of the rolling part is greater. This precession continues until the diameter of the roller and shelf cease to touch. At first H lifts with the shelf, and afterwards the shelf moving downwards is followed for some distance by the roller. If the tilt had been in the opposite direction the shelf D' would have acted upwards upon the roller H' and caused just the opposite kind of precession, and a moment of the opposite kind.

We now have the spindles out of their mid position; how are they brought back from O Q and O' Q' to O N and O' N', but with H permanently lowered just the right amount? It is the essence of Mr. Brennan's invention that after a restoring moment has been applied to the car the spindles shall go back to the position N O O' N' (with H permanently lowered), so as to be ready to act again. He effects this object in various ways. Some ways described in his patents are quite different from what he used on the model, and the method to be used on the full-size wagon will again be quite different. I will describe one of the methods. Mr. Brennan tells me that he considers this old method to be crude, but he is naturally unwilling to allow me to publish his latest method.

D' is a circular shelf extending from the mid position in my direction: D is a similar shelf extending from the mid position into the paper, or away from me. It is on these shelves that H' and H roll, causing precession away from N O O' N', as I have just described. When H' is inside the paper, or when H is outside the paper, they find no shelf to roll upon. There are, however, two other shelves L and L', for two other rollers M and M', which are attached to the frames concentric with the spindles; they are free to rotate, but are not rotated by spindles. When they are pressed by their shelves L or L' this causes negative precession, and they roll towards the N O O' N' position. There is, of course, friction at their supports, retarding their rotation, and therefore the precession. The important thing to remember is that

H and H', when they touch their shelves (when one is touching the other is not touching) cause a precession away from the mid position N O O' N' at the rate a, which produces a restoring moment ma of nearly constant amount (except for slipping), whereas where M or M' touches its shelf L or L' (when one is touching the other is not touching) the pressure on the shelf and friction determine the rate of the precession towards the mid position N O O' N', as well as the small vertical motion. The friction at the supports of M and M' is necessary.

Suppose that the tilt from the equilibrium position to be corrected is R, when D presses H upward. The moment ma, and its time of action (the total momental impulse) are too great, and R is over-corrected; this causes the roller M' to act on L', and the spindle return to the mid position; they go beyond the mid position, and now the roller H' acts on D', and there is a return to the mid position, and beyond it a little and so it goes on, the swings of the gyrostats out of and into the mid position, and the vibrations of the car about its position of equilibrium getting rapidly less and less until again neither H nor H', nor M nor M' is touching a shelf. It is indeed marvellous to see how rapidly the swings decay. Friction accelerates the precession away from N O O' N'. Friction retards the precession towards the middle position.

It will be seen that by using the two gyrostats instead of one when there is a curve on the line, although the plane N O O' N' rotates, and we may say that the gyrostats precess, the tilting couples which they might exercise are equal and opposite. I do not know if Mr. Brennan has tried a single gyrostat, the mid position of the axis of the wheel being vertical, but even in this case a change of slope, or inequalities in the line, might make it necessary to have a pair.

It is evident that this method of Mr. Brennan is altogether different in character from that of Mr. Schlick. Work is here actually done which must be supplied by the electro-motors.

One of the most important things to know is this: the Brennan model is wonderfully successful; the weight of the apparatus is not a large fraction of the weight of the wagon; will this also be the case with a car weighing 1,000 times as much? The calculation is not difficult, but I may not give it here. If we assume that suddenly the wagon finds itself at the angle R from its position of equilibrium, it may be taken that if the size of each dimension of the wagon be multiplied by n, and the size of each dimension of the apparatus be multiplied by p, then for a sudden gust of wind, or suddenly coming on a curve, or a sudden shift of position of part of the cargo, R may be taken as inversely proportional to n. I need not state the reasonable assumption which underlies this calculation, but the result is that if n is 10, p is 7.5. That is, if the weight of the wagon is multiplied by 1,000, the weight of the apparatus is only multiplied by 420. In fact, if, in the model, the weight of the apparatus is 10 per cent. of that of the wagon, in the large wagon the weight of the apparatus is only about 4 per cent. of that of the wagon. This is a very satisfactory result.[1]

My calculations seem to show that Mr. Schlick's apparatus will form a larger fraction of the whole weight of a ship, as the ship is larger, but in the present experimental stage of the subject it is unfair to say more than this seems probable. My own opinion is that large ships are sufficiently steady already.

In both cases it has to be remembered that if the *diameter* of the wheel can be increased in greater proportion than the dimensions of ship or wagon, the proportional weight of the apparatus may be diminished. A wheel of twice the diameter, but of the same weight, may have twice the moment of momentum, and may therefore be twice as effective. I assume the stresses in the material to be the same.

I have described Mr. Brennan's apparatus as used on his model. As applied to a full-sized wagon carrying many passengers, exhibited with great success in London, the arrangement is different, but I should have great difficulty in making the principle of its action clear without using mathematics.

---

[1] The weight of Mr. Brennan's loaded wagon is 313 lb., including gyrostats and storage cells. His two wheels weigh 13 lbs. If made of nickel steel and run at their highest safe speed they would weigh much less.

APPENDIX #11

APPENDIX #11

In page 64 I speak of the use of a gyrostat as a compass, but I did not dream that the gyro-compass would be in use within fifteen years. The errors of the magnetic compass on board ship are large and very troublesome, but they would not probably have compelled the adoption of the gyro-compass had it not been for the invention of the *submarine*. A magnetic compass cannot be used at all inside a steel submarine.

In page 62 the perfectly free gyrostat, whose spinning axis is at first horizontal and pointing due north, would seem gradually to tilt out of the horizontal if left free, and it would point away from the north. In truth the axis would really keep in a constant direction in space, and it is the direction of the north horizontal which is altering, due to the motion of the earth. To keep the axis pointing due north, it is necessary to keep it as nearly horizontal as possible, as is done in Fig. 47. As arranged in Fig. 47, the gyrostat on a firm support finds the due north quite rapidly if there is no friction about the vertical axis, and such a gyro-compass can be used on land.[1] I have used a very accurate one which comes to the north from any position in about half a minute. But on board ship it is not possible to get a firm support and hence the whole frame of Fig. 47 must be suspended on gymbals, which for stability must be above the centre of gravity of the whole suspended mass. In spite of the rolling and pitching of the

---

[1] The difficulty as to friction suggested to Lord Kelvin (*British Association Report*, 1884) that a float might be used to support the gyrostat, and this is the method actually employed in the compass used in the German Navy, and to some extent in our own Navy.

ship, gravity causes the average position of the spinning axis to be horizontal, as we wish it to be. If the axis is displaced from its position in the meridian it vibrates into and out of the position of no tilt with a very slow swing. The tilt is always very small, even for greater displacement in azimuth.

The directive torque towards the north is always exceedingly small, because of the slowness of the earth's rotation; it is proportional to the angular momentum of the wheel, and is less in higher latitudes. The wheel is usually inside a case which contains also the stator of a three-phase electric motor, so that the wheel keeps going at a constant great speed. The speed must not be so great as to cause dangerous stresses in its material due to centrifugal force. The wheel generates heat by friction against the atmosphere and its speed is limited by rise of temperature. The heat generated per second is proportional to the density of the atmosphere, and, therefore, in one kind of gyrocompass the case is filled with hydrogen, and in another there is air in a partly vacuous state. Inventors aim at getting great directive torque by using large and heavy wheels; they seem to forget that it might be better to diminish the resistance to motion about the vertical axis, which may roughly be called a solid friction. With large heavy wheels the expense is great and the friction is great. Again, the use of hydrogen or a partial vacuum introduces another possibility of failure due to accidents, and there are too many of these possibilities already.

The vibrations must be damped. It is usual for this purpose to introduce a torque about the vertical axis which is proportional to the tilt. This gives good damping, but unfortunately it introduces a considerable error which is different for different latitudes, and it also increases the error due to change of speed of the ship. It is better to damp the tilting vibration directly in the well-known simplest way, as this introduces no latitude error and does not increase the error to constant acceleration.

The error due to rolling and pitching and uniform acceleration of the ship; the latitude error; the serious "quadrantal error" due to the ship rolling when on a north-west or north-east course, and errors due to friction, have caused inventors to introduce numerous and complex methods of correction. It results that the binnacle of the gyro-compass is like a *bag-of-tricks*. It is enough to say that in that which is best known, as one part of the complexity, there are three gyrostats rotating in hydrogen. Still, it must be said for these unscientific contrivances that so long as they do not get out of order they are a help to navigators.

Mr. S. G. Brown proceeds in another way. He first invented a novel method of destruction of the solid friction about the vertical axis; he is therefore able to dispense with 95 per cent. of the directive torque hitherto supposed to be necessary; so he can use a small wheel rotating in the ordinary atmosphere.

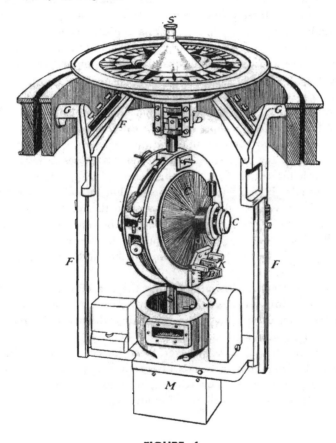

FIGURE 4

The frame F, Fig. 4, is supported on gimbals, of which one set G is shown. Moving relatively to this frame vertically and in azimuth is the ring R, which is rigidly fixed to the vertical spindle S, to which the compass card is attached. The case C contains the wheel, kept rotating on ball-bearings by means of a three-phase electric stator fixed in the case. C is supported by knife-edges E on the ring R, with which it is connected by weak springs. The swinging of C relatively to R is damped by the knife K, which cuts through cobbler's wax in the box B. Solid friction about the vertical spindle is destroyed in the following way. There is a three-phase motor in M which pumps oil underneath the spindle S, so that S rises and falls rapidly. There are three ring mercury contacts at D to convey current. The weak springs mentioned above exercise a torque which keeps the case S symmetrical with regard to the ring R. In his latest form Mr. Brown does away with these springs. He takes advantage of the fact that the case C contains air at a pressure greater than that of the atmosphere. A value carried by R directs this air through pipes so that a difference of pressure is maintained between two bottles containing oil attached to the other through a tube, so that the difference in their weights causes a torque tending to diminish the tilt of C. I call this positive torque. Another pair of bottles, smaller in size with much constriction in their connecting tube, receive air pressure in the opposite sense to that of the first pair. The negative torque is greatly delayed in its action, and consequently there is very efficient damping. This instrument has been subjected during the war to very severe tests in storms in the North Sea, and seems to have no errors.

Some important problems involving the use of gyrostats have been studied by many people during the war, with no great success. There is yet no compass, magnetic or gyrostatic, which can be relied upon for use on an airship or aeroplane.

Mr. S. G. Brown, has, however, been successful in producing an artificial horizon, that is, a mirror which keeps perfectly horizontal. It has long been wanted by seamen, who so seldom can get a clear horizon. It is yet more valuable for airmen.

CPSIA information can be obtained
at www.ICGtesting.com
Printed in the USA
LVHW08*1754180918
590551LV00016B/366/P